STAR CHEF RECIPES!

Queso Flameado (page 44)

STAR CHEF RECIPES!

90 DELICIOUS DISHES

Peach-Raspberry Crisp (page 149)

Contents

Meet the Chefs

Everyone who loves food can appreciate all that encompasses a great meal, from an early-morning breakfast all the way to a day-ending dessert. This cookbook has gathered recipes from some of the most renowned chefs in the world, with Mario Batali, Curtis Stone, Sandra Lee, Guy Fieri, Aarón Sánchez, Bobby Flay, Tyler Florence, Jamie Oliver, and many more offering delicious takes on food favorites. Get ready to take your dishes to the next level and cook like an all-star!

Lidia Bastianich

Lidia Bastianich is the author of seven previous books, five of which have been accompanied by a nationally-syndicated public television series. She is the owner of the New York City restaurant Felidia, among others, and she gives lectures on Italian cuisine throughout the country. She lives on Long Island, New York.

Mario Batali

Mario Batali counts 25 restaurants, ten cookbooks, numerous television shows, and three Eataly marketplaces among his ever-expanding empire of deliciousness. In April 2015, he opened Babbo Pizzeria e Enoteca, his first Boston project. The 8,700-square-foot restaurant, featuring wood-fired pizza, pasta, gelato, and more, is located on Beantown's famed Fan Pier waterfront district. He also opened the most well-received Eataly yet, Sao Paulo, Brazil, in May 2015.

Mario is the author of ten cookbooks, including the James Beard Award-Winning *Molto Italiano: 327 Simple Italian Recipes* (Ecco, 2005). His newest cookbook, *America Farm to Table: Simple, Delicious Recipes Celebrating Local Farmers* (Grand Central Life & Style), was released in October 2014. This book is an homage to farmers, the true rock stars of the food world. He appears daily on ABC's *The Chew*, a daytime talk show that celebrates and explores life through food. He and his co-hosts won their first Emmy for Best Talk Show Hosts in 2015.

Joy Bauer

Joy Bauer, MS, RDN, is one of the nation's leading health authorities. She is the nutrition and health expert for NBC's *TODAY Show*, the founder of Nourish Snacks, a monthly columnist for *Woman's Day*, and the New York City Ballet's official nutritionist. Joy is also the creator of JoyBauer.com and has authored several *New York Times* bestselling books, including *Food Cures*, *The Joy Fit Club*, *Slim & Scrumptious*, and *Your Inner Skinny*. Passionate about delivering scientifically sound, realistic information to millions, Joy believes it's never too early or too late to reap the benefits of healthy living. She resides in the New York area with her husband and three children.

The Beekman Boys
(Brent Ridge & Josh Kilmer-Purcell)

When **Josh Kilmer-Purcell** and **Dr. Brent Ridge** bought the Beekman Farm in upstate New York in 2008, they didn't just start a farm, they started a movement. Now they have a hit TV show, bestselling books, product lines, and a James Beard-nominated lifestyle website.

Known as *The Fabulous Beekman Boys* from their reality show on Cooking Channel, they are the authors of *The Beekman 1802 Heirloom Cookbook* and a memoir of their farm life, *The Bucolic Plague*. In 2012, millions watched as they went from "ultimate underdogs" to first-place winners on CBS's *The Amazing Race*.

John Besh

John Besh is a chef and native son dedicated to the culinary riches of southern Louisiana. Named by *Food & Wine* as one of the "Top 10 Best New Chefs in America," he won the coveted James Beard Foundation Award for Best Chef-Southeast in 2006 and was inducted into the Foundation's "Who's Who" in 2014. His twelve acclaimed restaurants each celebrate the bounty and traditions of the region.

Besh is the author of four award-winning cookbooks and host of two national public television cooking shows. The John Besh Foundation, founded in 2011, works to protect and preserve the culinary heritage and foodways of New Orleans. He and his wife, Jenifer, live with their four sons in southern Louisiana.

The Casserole Queens
(Crystal Cook & Sandy Pollock)

Part kitsch, part dish, all apron. Meet the **Casserole Queens**, Sandy Pollock and Crystal Cook. *New York Times* bestselling authors, Sandy and Crystal have taken their fresh-from-scratch meals from their home in Austin, Texas, to the stages of *Throwdown! with Bobby Flay, The TODAY Show*, QVC, and more. Featured on Epicurious, Oprah.com, and CNN.com, they've also been guests on Bobby Flay Radio on SiriusXM and Martha Stewart Living Radio on SiriusXM 110. In between speaking engagements, book signings, and cooking demonstrations, they're also earning a whole new legion of fans as stars of their own web series on the new YouTube food channel, HUNGRY.

Scott Conant

Scott Conant brings a deft touch and unwavering passion to creating singular dining experiences with soulful food and a convivial atmosphere. A graduate of the Culinary Institute of America, his career spans nearly 30 years, including multiple restaurants, an enthusiastic following of fans, and an ever-expanding brand.

He is the chef and owner of Scarpetta in Miami, Los Angeles, and Las Vegas, wine bar D.O.C.G. Enoteca, and the newly-opened Corsair at Turnberry Isle Miami. He also owns the SC Culinary Suite, a gorgeous private events space in SoHo, New York City. Scott has published three cookbooks, *New Italian Cooking, Bold Italian,* and *The Scarpetta Cookbook*, and frequently serves as a judge on Food Network's *Chopped*.

Rocco DiSpirito

Rocco DiSpirito is a James Beard award-winning chef, health advocate, and *New York Times* bestselling author. He is on a mission to prove that healthy and delicious are not mutually exclusive. Under his *Pound a Day* program, Rocco has personally coached, advised, and fed thousands of clients as they endeavor to reach a healthy weight. He serves as the Health Food Coach on ABC's primetime series *Extreme Weight Loss* and *Extreme Weight Loss: Love Can't Weight*. With a genuine passion for helping and advocating for those who struggle with food security and obesity, he makes charity work a top priority.

He is the author of eleven acclaimed cookbooks and his 3-Star restaurant, Union Pacific, was a culinary landmark in New York City for many years. When he's not cooking, Rocco enjoys bicycling and participating in triathlons.

Ree Drummond

Ree Drummond is the #1 *New York Times* bestselling author of *The Pioneer Woman Cooks, The Pioneer Woman Cooks: Food From My Frontier*, and *The Pioneer Woman Cooks: A Year of Holidays*. Ree's beloved website, The Pioneer Woman, was founded in 2006 and showcases her cooking, photography, and anecdotes about country life. Her top-rated cooking show, *The Pioneer Woman*, premiered on Food Network in 2011. Ree lives on a working cattle ranch in Oklahoma with her husband and four children.

Guy Fieri

Guy Fieri, chef, restaurateur, author, and host of Food Network's top-rated show *Diner, Drive-Ins and Dives*, began his love affair with food at the age of ten, selling soft pretzels from a three-wheeled bicycle cart he built with his father called "The Awesome Pretzel." In 1996, Guy launched his culinary career with the opening of Johnny Garlics, his first restaurant based in his hometown of Santa Rosa, California, with business partner Steve Gruber.

Since the opening of the first Johnny Garlics, Guy has gone on to create a culinary empire as a popular TV host, chef of six acclaimed restaurants, and *New York Times* bestselling cookbook author. In 2006, Guy premiered his first show, *Guy's Big Bite*, on Food Network. Today, this "culinary rock star" guest judges on *Food Network Star* and collaborates with Rachael Ray in the star-studded competition series, *Rachael vs. Guy Celebrity Cook-Off*, which premiered in January 2012 on Food Network.

Bobby Flay

Bobby Flay, *New York Times* bestselling author, is the chef-owner of five fine-dining restaurants, including Gato, Bar Americain, Mesa Grill, and Bobby Flay Steak, and an expanding roster of Bobby's Burger Palaces. He is the host of numerous popular cooking shows on Food Network—from the Emmy-winning *Bobby Flay's Barbecue Addiction* to *Iron Chef America*, *Throwdown! with Bobby Flay*, and *Food Network Star*—as well as *Brunch @ Bobby's* on Cooking Channel.

Tyler Florence

Tyler Florence is a television star, author of twelve books, product designer, and chef-owner of Wayfare Tavern in San Francisco and El Paseo in Mill Valley, California. He hosts *Tyler's Ultimate* and *The Great Food Truck Race* on Food Network. He produces wine under his California Crush label and opened the Tyler Florence Test Kitchen—a culinary lab, think tank, and event space—in 2014. He lives in California with his wife and three children.

Gale Gand

Gale Gand is a pastry chef and partner of the new restaurant Spritz Burger, a collaboration with The Hearty Boys, and partner in the Michelin one-star restaurant Tru, both in Chicago. She was the host of Food Network's long-running show *Sweet Dreams* and is the author of eight cookbooks. Gale teaches cooking classes all over the country and is an artisanal soda pop maker, producing Gale's Root Beer, which is sold nationally. She has received two James Beard Awards, been inducted into the Chicago Chefs Hall of Fame, and is the mother of three.

Lorena García

Venezuelan-born restaurateur, TV personality, and cookbook author **Lorena García** is currently one of the country's leading chefs. She is well known for numerous TV series (*Top Chef Masters, Top Chef Estrellas, Sazon con Lorena García, Lorena en Su Salsa,* and *El Mejor De Los Peores*, to name a few), a successful chain of restaurants, and her cookbook, *Lorena García's New Latin Classics.* She was the creator of the Cantina Bell menu at Taco Bell, and has her own cookware line, Lorena Bella Kitchen Collection, for HSN.

Carla Hall

Carla Hall is a co-host on ABC's popular lifestyle series *The Chew*. She is best known as a competitor on Bravo's *Top Chef*, where she won over audiences with her fun catch phrase, "Hootie Hoo," and her philosophy to always cook with love. Carla's approach to cooking blends her classic French training and southern upbringing for a twist on traditional favorites. She is committed to health and balance in everyday living.

Her first restaurant, Carla Hall's Southern Kitchen, opened in New York City in 2015. She is also the owner of Carla Hall Petite Cookies, an artisan cookie company. Her newest cookbook, *Carla's Comfort Food: Favorites Dishes from Around the World* was published in April 2014, and her first cookbook, *Cooking with Love: Comfort Food That Hugs You*, recently re-released in paperback.

Donna Hay

At the age of eight, **Donna Hay** skipped into a kitchen, picked up a mixing bowl, and never looked back. She later moved to the world of magazine test kitchens and publishing, where she established her trademark style of simple, smart, and seasonal recipes.

Her unique style turned her into an international food-publishing phenomenon as a bestselling author of 23 cookbooks, publisher of the bi-monthly *donna hay magazine* and number one iPad app in Australia, newspaper columnist, creator of the donna hay for Royal Doulton Homewares collection, and owner of her online store. Donna is a working mom to two beautiful boys. Her first television series, *Donna Hay—fast, fresh, simple.*, brought her approach to food to life for viewers in over 32 countries.

Ingrid Hoffmann

Originally from Colombia, **Ingrid Hoffmann** developed a love for cooking as a child during the time she spent in the kitchen with her mother, a Cordon Bleu-trained chef. As a teenager, she worked in her mom's catering and restaurant business. Upon moving to Miami, they opened a restaurant together. As host of *Delicioso* on Univision and *Simply Delicioso* on the Cooking Channel, Ingrid has become arguably the foremost Latin authority on cooking and lifestyle, and her Delicioso brand has become one of the most recognizable, trusted, and entertaining food brands for Hispanic America. In 2011, Ingrid was named Flavors of Passion Master Chef of the Year—an award that was created and designed to honor the nation's best Latino chefs.

Stephanie Izard

Celebrated chef and author **Stephanie Izard** is the chef-partner of Chicago restaurants Girl & the Goat and Little Goat. Her accolades include the 2013 James Beard Award for "Best Chef: Great Lakes," "2011 *Food & Wine* Best New Chef," and winner of *Top Chef* season four. Her first book, *Girl in the Kitchen*, was published by Chronicle in 2011. In the summer of 2015, she opened her third restaurant, a Chinese concept called Duck Duck Goat, in Chicago's West Loop neighborhood.

You can find out more about Stephanie at stephanieizard.com, or follow her on Twitter @StephAndTheGoat.

Clinton Kelly

Clinton Kelly is the Emmy Award-winning co-host of ABC's daytime hit *The Chew*. He also co-hosted *What Not to Wear*, TLC's longest-running primetime reality show, for a decade. His new show, *Love at First Swipe*, premiered on TLC in October 2015.

Clinton is both a contributing editor and monthly columnist for *Woman's Day* magazine and has authored the books *Freakin' Fabulous, Freakin' Fabulous on a Budget*, and *Oh, No She Didn't*. His clothing line, Kelly by Clinton Kelly, is sold on QVC and his tabletop housewares line, Effortless Table, is available at Macys.com. His partnership with Macy's began in 2005, and he's since appeared in high-profile national television commercials, consulted on private label, ready-to-wear brands, conducted over 100 style seminars across the United States, and launched interactive social media campaigns.

Katie Lee

Katie Lee learned the value of using seasonal ingredients by cooking alongside her Grandma Dora with fresh vegetables from her grandpa's garden and meat from her family's cattle and pig farms. Today, Katie is a co-host on Food Network's *The Kitchen* and the author of three cookbooks, *Endless Summer Cookbook, The Comfort Table* and *The Comfort Table: Recipes for Everyday Occasions*. Katie also writes a column for *SELF* and published her first novel, *Groundswell*, in 2011. She sits on the Celebrity Board for Feeding America and the Culinary Council of Food Bank for New York City. When not working or volunteering, she enjoys surfing, traveling, and playing with her pug, Fionula. She resides in the Hamptons and Tribeca.

Sandra Lee

Sandra Lee, a multi-Emmy and Gracie Award winner, is an internationally acclaimed expert in all things lifestyle. She is the editor-in-chief of *Sandra Lee Magazine* and sandralee.com. As the host of multiple hit television shows on The Food Network, HGTV, and The Cooking Channel, Sandra became a household name, and her user-friendly approach connected with audiences in 63 countries.

In May 2015, at age 48, Sandra publically shared her breast cancer diagnosis and urged women to take charge of their health by getting screened. She is committed to continuing her advocacy through Stand Up To Cancer and Susan G. Komen, among others. In September 2015, Sandra was honored on Capitol Hill with the Excellence in Cancer Awareness Award. She is a founding member of UNICEF®'s Board of Directors, Los Angeles chapter and also served an extended term as the national spokesperson for the No Kid Hungry Campaign. She works nationally with Citymeals-on-Wheels and food banks across America.

Since 2002, Sandra has written 27 cookbooks, including a memoir, *Made From Scratch*, and a novel, *The Recipe Box*.

Lisa Lillien (Hungry Girl)

Lisa Lillien (a.k.a. Hungry Girl) has turned her appetite for better-for-you food finds, recipes, and swaps into a multimedia phenomenon. Lisa has a fan base of over two million daily email subscribers (hungry-girl.com) and social media followers, a super-successful book series with ten *New York Times* bestsellers, and a cooking show that airs on both Food Network and Cooking Channel. Her realistic approach to eating has shown hungry people everywhere that they can eat the foods they crave and still fit into their favorite jeans. Lisa is not a nutritionist, a dietitian, or a doctor. She's just hungry . . .

Julie Morris

New York Times bestselling author **Julie Morris** is a natural food chef, writer, educator, and advocate of whole, plant-based foods and superfoods for optimal health. Based in Los Angeles, Julie has traveled the United States and abroad to share her cutting-edge nutritional expertise. Her in-depth knowledge of superfoods has been quoted by *The Wall Street Journal*, *GQ*, and *Women's Health Magazine*, as well as featured in numerous culinary publications. The recipes and nutrition tips in her four authoritative superfood cookbooks are dedicated to making a vibrantly healthy lifestyle both easy to achieve and delicious to follow.

Jamie Oliver

Jamie Oliver is an internationally-acclaimed chef, TV host, bestselling cookbook author, restaurateur, and food activist. Born in London, his career accelerated after the premiere of his hit show, *The Naked Chef*. From there, he opened his restaurant Fifteen in London, which is run by his charity, the Jamie Oliver Food Foundation. The foundation, as well as his annual Food Revolution Day, campaign for nutritious school meals, healthy lifestyle changes, and overall better food education.

Apart from his other restaurants, Barbecoa and Jamie's Italian, Jamie writes for his own *Jamie Magazine* and appears on the YouTube channels Jamie Oliver's Food Tube and Drinks Tube. His newest cookbook, *Everyday Super Food*, was published in October 2015. He lives in London and Essex with his wife and four children.

Daphne Oz

Daphne Oz is a chef, *New York Times* bestselling author, and Emmy Award-winning co-host of ABC's *The Chew*. She earned her bachelor's degree from Princeton University before attending the Institute for Integrative Nutrition and the Natural Gourmet Institute. Her food philosophy is that every meal should be a celebration of happy and healthy, and her books focus on easy lifestyle solutions for doing little things a little bit better for a more delicious, full, and fun life. She lives with her husband, John, and their children in New York City.

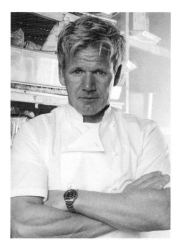

Gordon Ramsay

Gordon Ramsay is a multi-Michelin starred chef and restaurateur. Internationally-renowned, he has opened a string of successful restaurants across the globe. He has become a recognizable television personality, with hit shows on FOX—most notably, *Kitchen Nightmares*, *Hell's Kitchen*, *MasterChef*, and *MasterChef Junior*—as well as in the UK. He has also published several books, many of which are international bestsellers, including his autobiography, *Roasting in Hell's Kitchen*.

In 2014, Gordon and his wife Tana set up the Gordon and Tana Ramsay Foundation to make a meaningful difference to causes that are important to them. He lives with Tana and their four children, along with their bulldog Rumpole and two cats. He divides his time between Los Angeles and South London.

Carolyne Roehm

Style icon and lifestyle maven **Carolyne Roehm** has been part of American design culture for over four decades. With a career spanning fashion, gardening, entertaining, publishing, and decorative arts, Carolyne's energy in seeking her next challenge knows no bounds. Finding a mentor in Oscar de la Renta, Carolyne worked alongside the couture great for 10 years before launching her own fashion house in 1985. A discerning eye and passion for beauty led her into the world of flowers, where her books are often referred to as the best in their field. Now the author of 12 books, Carolyne's mission is to teach others how to capture and create beauty in their lives, in both the everyday and the extraordinary.

Marcus Samuelsson

Marcus Samuelsson is the youngest person to ever receive a three-star review from *The New York Times*. He has won multiple James Beard Foundation Awards, including "Best Chef: New York City," and was tasked with planning and executing the Obama Administration's first State dinner. He was also crowned champion of television shows *Top Chef Masters* and *Chopped All Stars*. He serves as a mentor on ABC's *The Taste* and stars in FYI's *The Feed*.

Samuelsson is co-producer of Harlem EatUp! and is the author of the *New York Times* bestselling memoir *Yes, Chef*, as well as several cookbooks including his newest, *Marcus Off Duty: The Recipes I Cook at Home*, which was published in October 2014. In spring 2015, he opened his second Harlem restaurant, Streetbird Rotisserie, a kitchenette, followed by Marcus', in Hamilton, Bermuda.

Aarón Sánchez

Aarón Sánchez is Chef/Partner of Johnny Sánchez, with locations in Baltimore and New Orleans. He is a judge on Food Network's hit series *Chopped*, and the host of Cooking Channel's Emmy-nominated *Taco Trip*. Aarón has received a James Beard Award and appeared at the White House as a guest chef. He has authored two books, *Simple Food, Big Flavor* and *La Comida del Barrio*.

Aarón is an ambassador for Food Bank NYC and Why Hunger? and is a Chef Mentor for the scholarship program Chefs Move!

Aarón's creativity extends far beyond the kitchen—he is a partner at the legendary Daredevil Tattoo in New York City, home to the country's premiere tattoo museum. He is an avid music lover and enjoys cooking to the sounds of Alabama Shakes, Amos Lee, and Lenny Kravitz.

Curtis Stone

Curtis Stone is an internationally-known chef, award-winning restaurateur, TV host, and *New York Times* bestselling author. Born in Melbourne, Australia, he discovered his passion for food watching his grandmother, Maude, make her legendary fudge. He honed his skills in the UK under three-star Michelin genius, Marco Pierre White. While living in London, Curtis appeared in several UK cooking shows before catching the eye of television producers in Australia and the US. In February 2014, he opened his first solo restaurant in Beverly Hills. Named after his grandmother, Maude Restaurant has garnered rave reviews from James Beard Foundation (2015 Best New Restaurant semifinalist), *TIME/Travel & Leisure* (lists Maude as one of the best new restaurants in the world), and *LA Weekly* (2014 Best New Restaurant and 2015 Best Restaurant).

Michael Symon

Michael Symon (@chefsymon) cooks with soul. Growing up in a Greek and Sicilian family, the Cleveland native creates boldly flavored, deeply satisfying dishes at his restaurants in America's heartland. He also shares his exuberant, approachable cooking style and infectious laugh with viewers as an Iron Chef on Food Network and as a co-host on ABC's *The Chew*. Michael is the chef and owner of more than twelve restaurants, including Mabel's BBQ, which opened in late 2015 in downtown Cleveland. He recently debuted his own line of knives and released his fourth cookbook, *5 in 5 For Every Season*, in fall 2015.

The Tippling Bros.
(Tad Carducci & Paul Tanguay)

Since 2007, the **Tippling Bros.** (Tad Carducci and Paul Tanguay) have consulted on spirits and mixology for hundreds of bars, restaurants, hotels, and beverage brands, both nationally and globally, creating cocktails, designing bars, executing events, training and educating, developing flavors, and hosting consumer cocktail classes. They are partners in a cocktail bar appropriately named The Tippler, located in Manhattan's Chelsea Market. They have received numerous awards and accolades for their work, and they (or their cocktails) have been featured in a myriad of print, online, radio, and TV media outlets. They released their first cocktail book, *The Tippling Bros.' A Lime and a Shaker: Discovering Mexican-Inspired Cocktails*, in April 2015.

Marcela Valladolid

Marcela Valladolid is a celebrity chef, television personality, designer, author, and businesswoman. She began her professional career as a Food Editor for *Bon Appetite* magazine, and published her first book, *Fresh Mexico,* in 2009. She hosted *Mexican Made Easy* for Food Network in 2010 and released a companion book, *Mexican Made Easy*, in 2011. In 2013, she launched her own line of food products in partnership with Safeway. She also has her own line of organic tequila, Hacienda de la Flor.

Marcela has been featured in numerous print publications, such as *The Wall Street Journal* and *Food & Wine* magazine, and has appeared on several national television shows, such as *The TODAY SHOW, The Talk, The Chew, The View, The Rachael Ray Show,* and more. She is currently a co-host on the Emmy-nominated hit show, *The Kitchen*, on Food Network. She continues to use her career and bicultural upbringing to reach both general and Hispanic audiences. She is the mother of two wonderful boys, Fausto and David.

Spiced Cranberry Coffee Cake (page 32)

Breakfast & Brunch

Wake up to the aromas and flavors of these comforting and delicious recipes from some of your favorite chefs. John Besh's Stuffed French Toast and Curtis Stone's Hotcakes with Delicious Blueberry Compote are just two ways to start your day off right.

John Besh's
Stuffed French Toast

Total time 25 minutes

Makes 4 two-piece servings

1 **(13-oz.) jar Nutella**	**1** **c. milk**	**½ tsp. vanilla extract**
16 slices good white bread	**½ c. sugar**	**1** **pinch salt**
(2 slices per person)	**¼ c. orange juice**	**¼ c. canola oil**
6 **eggs, beaten**	**4** **Tbsp. butter, melted**	

1   Spread 1 tablespoon of Nutella between 2 slices of bread, forming 8 sandwiches. Invert a large water glass over each sandwich and press down to get 1 clean circle from each, cutting away the crusts and sealing the sandwich.

2   Mix together the eggs, milk, sugar, orange juice, butter, vanilla, and salt in a large shallow bowl. Dip the sandwiches in the egg mixture until they are well covered. Do this in small batches, because you'll cook the French toast immediately after each egg dip.

3   Heat 2 tablespoons of canola oil on a griddle or in a large skillet over medium heat. Add half the sandwiches and cook, turning once, until browned on both sides. Repeat with the remaining canola oil and sandwiches. Serve immediately.

Each serving About 782 calories, 18g protein, 79g carbohydrate, 44g total fat (22g saturated), 4g fiber, 316mg cholesterol, 557mg sodium

"Nutella is a chocolate hazelnut spread in a jar, created in Italy in the 1940s, and when my wife and I were living in Europe, we became hooked on it. But the truth is, I'll stuff French toast with anything, from peanut butter and honey to apricot preserves, and the dish is always a hit."

—John Besh

Katie Lee's Cinnamon-Swirl Breakfast Bread Pudding

Total time 50 minutes plus chilling

Makes 4 servings

4 eggs	1 tsp. cinnamon	Nonstick cooking spray
1½ c. milk	½ loaf day-old bread,	Maple syrup, for serving
3 Tbsp. brown sugar	cut into cubes	
1 tsp. vanilla extract	¼ c. pecans, chopped	

Berries with Honey-Lime Yogurt Sauce

Place **3 c. mixed berries** (raspberries, blueberries, blackberries, or strawberries) in a serving bowl. In a small bowl, combine **1 c. plain yogurt**, **3 Tbsp. honey**, and **½ tsp. lime zest**. Serve berries drizzled with yogurt sauce. Garnish with **mint**, if you want.

1 In a large bowl, whisk eggs and milk. Add the brown sugar, vanilla extract, and cinnamon, and whisk until all the ingredients are completely incorporated. Stir the bread and pecans into the egg mixture. Coat an 8" by 8" baking pan with nonstick cooking spray. Pour in the bread pudding, and cover with foil. Let sit in the refrigerator at least one hour, or up to overnight.

2 Preheat oven to 350°F. Bake the bread pudding, covered, for 30 minutes. Remove the foil and bake an additional 10 minutes, until the pudding is browned. Serve with hot maple syrup.

Each serving About 358 calories, 14g protein, 42g carbohydrate, 14g total fat (4g saturated), 2g fiber, 195mg cholesterol, 371mg sodium

Gale Gand's
Broccoli and Ham Strata

Total time 1 hour plus chilling   **Makes 8 servings**

5 c. cubed French bread	1 tsp. salt	½ c. cubed ham
10 eggs	½ c. broccoli florets	½ c. diced red pepper, sautéed
4 c. milk	½ c. red skinned potatoes,	2 c. grated sharp Cheddar
1 tsp. dry mustard	cooked and quartered	cheese

1   Butter a 9" by 13" baking dish. Place bread cubes in the dish, and then top with the vegetables, ham, and grated cheese. In a bowl, whisk together the eggs, milk, dry mustard, and salt. Pour the mixture over the bread cubes. Fold it in slightly to mix in the vegetables and ham. Cover and chill up to 24 hours, to let it soak up the custard.

2   Preheat the oven to 350°F. Uncover the dish and bake for 60 minutes. Tent with foil if the dish is browning too quickly. Serve immediately.

Each serving About 378 calories, 23g protein, 24g carbohydrate, 21g total fat (11g saturated), 1g fiber, 275mg cholesterol, 849mg sodium

Curtis Stone's Hotcakes with Delicious Blueberry Compote

Total time 55 minutes

Makes 4 servings

Blueberry Compote
- 18 oz. fresh blueberries
- ¼ c. sugar
- Grated zest and juice of 1 lemon
- ¼ c. coarsely chopped fresh mint leaves (optional)

Hotcakes
- 1 c. fresh ricotta cheese
- 4 large eggs, separated
- ¾ c. buttermilk, shaken
- 1 c. all-purpose flour
- 1½ tsp. baking powder
- Pinch salt
- ¼ c. sugar
- ½ c. fresh blueberries
- About 3 Tbsp. unsalted butter
- Butter, for serving

1 Make the Blueberry Compote: Combine the blueberries, sugar, lemon zest, and 2 tablespoons of the lemon juice in a medium saucepan over medium heat and cook for 2 minutes, or until the sugar dissolves. (Don't let the berries cook too long or they will become mushy and lose their beautiful shape.) Remove from the heat. Gently stir in the chopped mint, if using. Keep warm.

2 Make the Hotcakes: Whisk the ricotta and the egg yolks together in a large bowl; then whisk in the buttermilk. Sift the flour, baking powder, and salt into the ricotta mixture. Stir with a whisk until just combined.

3 Using an electric mixer, beat the egg whites and sugar in a large bowl until stiff peaks form. Using a large rubber spatula, gently fold the egg whites through the batter in 2 batches. Gently fold the fresh blueberries into the batter.

4 Melt some butter on a hot griddle pan over medium-low heat. Ladle the batter onto the griddle (you should be able to fit 3 hotcakes at a time) and cook for about 3 minutes per side, or until the hotcakes puff, become golden brown, and are just cooked through.

5 Transfer the hotcakes to plates. Spoon the warm blueberry compote over the hotcakes, and then top with a dollop of butter. Serve immediately.

Each serving About 636 calories, 19g protein, 76g carbohydrate, 30g total fat (17g saturated), 4g fiber, 261mg cholesterol, 411mg sodium

The Casserole Queens'
Spiced Cranberry Coffee Cake

Total time 1 hour 15 minutes   **Makes 12 servings**

¾ c. (1½ sticks) unsalted butter, at room temp., plus more for pan

3 c. all-purpose flour, plus more for pan

1½ tsp. baking powder

1½ tsp. baking soda

1 tsp. kosher salt

1½ c. granulated sugar

3 large eggs

1½ c. low-fat buttermilk

2 tsp. grated orange zest

2 c. Spiced Cranberries or store-bought cranberry sauce

1 c. walnuts, roughly chopped

1¼ c. confectioners' sugar

3 Tbsp. milk

Spiced Cranberries

In a medium saucepan, bring **2 c. each water and sugar** to a boil. Add **4 c. fresh or frozen cranberries, 2 tsp. ground cinnamon, 1 tsp. ground cloves, ½ tsp. ground nutmeg,** and **¼ tsp. grated orange zest** and boil until the skins burst, about 7 minutes. Reduce heat and simmer, covered, for 1 hour. Remove from heat and let cool.

1 Heat oven to 350°F. Coat a 9" by 13" baking dish with butter and lightly dust with flour. In a medium bowl, whisk together the flour, baking powder, baking soda, and salt.

2 Using an electric mixer, beat the butter and granulated sugar in a large bowl until light and fluffy, about 3 minutes. Beat in the eggs, then the buttermilk and orange zest. Reduce the mixer speed to low and gradually add the flour mixture, mixing just until incorporated.

3 Spread half the batter into the prepared baking dish. Dollop 1 cup Spiced Cranberries over the top, then gently spread, swirling into the batter. Top with the remaining batter, then dollop with the remaining cranberries.

4 Sprinkle the walnuts over the top and bake until the cake is golden brown and a pick inserted into the center comes out clean, 45 to 50 minutes. Let cool for 5 minutes.

5 While the cake cools, make the icing: In a small bowl, whisk together the confectioners' sugar and milk until smooth. Drizzle the icing over the warm cake, then let cool completely before serving.

Each serving About 534 calories, 8g protein, 82g carbohydrate, 20g total fat (9g saturated), 2g fiber, 79mg cholesterol, 449mg sodium

"Having coffee cake on hand is perfect when hosting out-of-town guests. Everyone can ease into the morning with a cup of joe and a slice of cake—no need to make a big fuss over breakfast."

—Crystal and Sandy

Marcus Samuelsson's Mushroom, Goat Cheese, and Tomato Tart

Total time 1 hour 30 minutes plus standing and cooling **Makes 8 servings**

½ c. plus 2 Tbsp. olive oil
1 c. sliced button mushrooms
½ c. sliced portobello
   mushrooms
½ c. sliced shiitake mushrooms
8 cloves garlic, halved
   lengthwise
¼ c. balsamic vinegar

8 oil-packed sun-dried
   tomatoes, drained and halved
   lengthwise
6 to 12 anchovy fillets, coarsely
   chopped
¼ c. pitted Kalamata or Niçoise
   olives, chopped
1 tsp. fresh thyme leaves

2 small-to-medium Idaho russet
   or other baking potatoes,
   unpeeled
1 unbaked 10-in. tart shell
Kosher salt and freshly ground
   black pepper
6 oz. fresh goat cheese

1 In a large skillet, heat 2 tablespoons olive oil over medium-high heat. Add all of the mushrooms and garlic and sauté for 10 to 15 minutes, or until the mushrooms are golden brown. Remove from the heat.

2 In a bowl, combine the mushrooms and garlic, remaining ½ cup olive oil, vinegar, tomatoes, anchovies, olives, and thyme; mix well. Cover and let stand at room temperature for 2 hours.

3 After the mushrooms have stood for about 1 hour, preheat the oven to 400°F. Poke the potatoes in a few places with a fork and bake for 40 minutes, or until they offer only a little resistance in the center when pierced with a thin-bladed knife. Remove from the oven and let cool slightly. Reduce the oven temperature to 375°F.

4 When the potatoes are cool enough to handle, peel and slice into ½-inch-thick rounds. Layer the potato slices in the bottom of the tart shell, seasoning them generously with salt and pepper. Drain the mushroom mixture in a sieve held over a bowl to capture the marinade. Spread the mushroom mixture over the potatoes. Crumble the goat cheese evenly over the top.

5 Bake the tart for 20 to 25 minutes, or until the cheese begins to turn golden. Remove from the oven, let cool on a wire rack, and serve warm or at room temperature. Drizzle with a few tablespoons of the reserved marinade just before serving.

Each serving About 409 calories, 8g protein, 27g carbohydrate, 30g total fat (8g saturated), 2g fiber, 13mg cholesterol, 496mg sodium

The Beekman Boys'
Mini Ham and Cheese Biscuits

Total time 40 minutes plus cooling   **Makes 24 biscuits**

2 c. all-purpose flour, spooned and leveled	5 Tbsp. cold unsalted butter, cut into bits	1 tsp. Dijon mustard
2 tsp. baking powder	1 c. (4 oz.) shredded sharp Cheddar cheese	½ c. hot pepper jelly
¼ tsp. baking soda	¾ c. buttermilk	6 slices smoked ham (about ¼ lb.), quartered
½ tsp. salt		

1 Preheat the oven to 425°F. Line a baking sheet with parchment paper.

2 In a large bowl, whisk together the flour, baking powder, baking soda, and salt. With a pastry blender or two knives used scissors fashion, cut the butter into the flour mixture until pea-sized lumps remain. Add the cheese and stir to combine. With a fork, mix in the buttermilk and mustard until combined. The mixture will not form a ball but will stick together when pinched.

3 Turn the dough out onto a lightly floured work surface and roll out ½-inch thick. With a 1½-inch biscuit cutter, cut out 24 rounds, rerolling scraps as necessary. Place on the lined baking sheet and bake for 17 to 20 minutes, or until golden brown and set.

4 Let cool on a rack. Split the biscuits in half horizontally. Top the bottom half with 1 teaspoon jelly and 1 piece of ham. Replace the top of the biscuit.

Each biscuit About 100 calories, 3g protein, 12g carbohydrate, 4g total fat (3g saturated), 0g fiber, 14mg cholesterol, 194mg sodium

Variations

Give the biscuits a little crunch by reducing the flour by 2 Tbsp. and adding **2 Tbsp. cornmeal.**

For an even richer biscuit, swap in **heavy cream** for the buttermilk, increase the baking powder to 2½ tsp., and omit the baking soda.

Stuffed Mushrooms (page 41)

Appetizers

Every good meal deserves a stand-up opening act, and these recipes are the perfect starters. Try out Daphne Oz's Stuffed Mushrooms or The Casserole Queens' Queso Flameado—you can't go wrong with any of these crowd-pleasing apps.

Aarón Sánchez's
Shrimp Tostadas with Salsa

Total time 30 minutes

Makes 6 servings

1   lb. uncooked medium or large shrimp, peeled and deveined
2   tsp. extra-virgin olive oil
1   Tbsp. ground ancho chile powder (or whatever chile powder you have)
½   tsp. ground coriander
½   tsp. ground cumin
Salt and pepper, to taste
1   c. plum tomatoes, diced
½   avocado, diced
1   Tbsp. fresh cilantro, chopped
1   serrano chile, finely minced
½   c. cucumber, seeded, peeled, and finely diced
½   c. red onion, finely diced
1   Tbsp. fresh lime juice
6   (4-in.-diameter) fried corn tortillas

1   Mix the shrimp, oil, chile powder, coriander, and cumin in a bowl. Season with salt and pepper, and mix well.

2   Make Aaron's Salsa: Mix tomatoes, avocado, cilantro, chile, cucumber, red onion, and lime juice in a small bowl. Add salt and pepper.

3   Heat a large nonstick skillet over high heat. Coat the pan with olive oil, add seasoned shrimp, and sauté until just cooked through, about 3 minutes.

4   Spoon salsa on each tostada. Top with shrimp.

Each serving About 175 calories, 16g protein, 11g carbohydrate, 7g total fat (1g saturated), 3g fiber, 120mg cholesterol, 215mg sodium

Marcela Valladolid's
Party-Perfect Guacamole

Total time 35 minutes plus cooling   **Makes 4 servings**

1 **(2-lb.) head cauliflower or Romanesco, sliced into cross-sections or cut into 1½-in.-wide florets**	1 **tsp. dried oregano, preferably Mexican**	4 **oz. (½ c.) cream cheese, at room temp.**
3 **Tbsp. olive oil**	**Salt and freshly ground black pepper**	1 **serrano chile, stemmed, deveined, and seeded**
	1 **Haas avocado from Mexico, peeled and pitted**	½ **c. chopped fresh cilantro**
		1 **Tbsp. fresh lime juice**

1   Preheat the oven to 400°F.

2   Put the cauliflower, oil, and oregano in a large bowl. Sprinkle with salt and pepper and toss to combine. Spread in a single layer on large baking sheet and roast, turning occasionally, until tender and golden brown, about 30 minutes. Let cool and then transfer to platter.

3   Meanwhile, in the bowl of a food processor, or in a blender, combine the avocado, cream cheese, serrano, cilantro, and lime juice and blend until smooth and creamy, about 1 minute. Season with salt and pepper. Transfer to a small bowl and serve with the cauliflower for dipping.

Each serving About 292 calories, 5g protein, 11g carbohydrate, 27g total fat (8g saturated), 5g fiber, 31mg cholesterol, 258mg sodium

"I make this delicious dip during awards season and it's always a big hit," says Marcela, who serves it with roasted cauliflower. "But it works any time of year since avocados from Mexico are available fresh year-round."

Daphne Oz's Stuffed Mushrooms

Total time 55 minutes

Makes 30 mushrooms

- 4 Tbsp. olive oil
- 30 button mushrooms (about 1 lb.), wiped with damp paper towels, stems finely chopped, and caps removed
- 3 Tbsp. minced shallots
- 3 Tbsp. blanched almonds, chopped
- 2 garlic cloves, minced
- ¾ tsp. kosher salt
- ¼ tsp. hot red pepper flakes
- 6 Tbsp. chopped flat-leaf parsley
- 1½ Tbsp. herbes de Provence or dried thyme
- 3 Tbsp. whole wheat panko breadcrumbs
- 3 Tbsp. vegetable stock or water
- 1½ tsp. grated lemon zest
- 1½ Tbsp. fresh lemon juice
- 3 Tbsp. Pecorino Romano cheese, grated
- ½ c. pomegranate seeds, for garnish

1 Heat oven to 375°F.

2 In a small nonstick skillet, heat 1 tablespoon oil over medium heat. Add chopped mushroom stems and shallots and cook, stirring frequently, 3 minutes, until lightly browned. Add almonds, garlic, salt, and pepper flakes. Cook, stirring frequently, 2 minutes. Remove from heat. Stir in 4 tablespoons of the parsley, herbes de Provence, and breadcrumbs.

3 Scrape mushroom mixture into a food processor; add stock, lemon zest, and lemon juice. Pulse until well blended.

4 In a large bowl, toss mushroom caps with remaining 3 tablespoons oil. Fill each with 1 tablespoon of the mushroom mixture. Place caps, filling-side up, on a rimmed baking sheet, about 1 inch apart. Sprinkle cheese over filling. Bake 20 to 25 minutes, until cheese browns a little and mushrooms are hot and cooked through. Sprinkle with remaining 2 tablespoons parsley; garnish with pomegranate seeds.

Each serving (3 mushrooms) About 99 calories, 4g protein, 6g carbohydrate, 7g total fat (1g saturated), 2g fiber, 3mg cholesterol, 213mg sodium

Daphne calls these her "gateway" vegetarian appetizer: "Even meat-eaters find them decadent," she says.

Carolyne Roehm's
Summer Rice Croquettes

Total time 25 minutes plus cooling and frying   **Makes about 48 croquettes**

2 c. Arborio rice, uncooked
2 Tbsp. olive oil
1 c. white wine
5 c. chicken stock
1 c. Parmigiano-Reggiano cheese
1 Tbsp. butter
½ c. onions, minced

2 stalks celery, finely diced
2 carrots, finely diced
2 ears corn, cob cut off
4 Tbsp. sun-dried tomatoes, cut into small bits
2 cloves garlic, minced
½ c. chopped parsley
Salt and pepper, to taste

½ lb. mozzarella cheese, cut into ½-in. cubes
1 c. all-purpose flour
2 eggs, lightly whipped
1 c. fine breadcrumbs
Canola oil, for frying

1   Sauté rice in olive oil; add wine and reduce. Add hot chicken stock a little at a time, stirring constantly for about 18 minutes, or until rice is al dente. Turn off heat; stir in Parmigiano-Reggiano and butter and let cool.

2   In a frying pan, sauté all vegetables and garlic until soft, about 5 to 7 minutes. Add parsley, salt, and pepper; mix gently and thoroughly into rice.

3   To shape croquettes, wet hands, take 2 tablespoons rice (a small ice cream scoop works well), and shape into a ball. Make an indentation in the center and push in a piece of mozzarella. Smooth rice over cheese and reshape into a ball.

4   Roll each ball in flour, shake off excess, dip in egg, and roll in breadcrumbs. Place on cookie sheet until all are made. Keep cold. They can be made in advance until ready to fry.

5   Deep fry croquettes in hot oil and place on paper towels. Keep warm in 200°F oven and serve.

Each serving (4 croquettes) About 390 calories, 14g protein, 48g carbohydrate, 16g total fat (5g saturated), 3g fiber, 56mg cholesterol, 786mg sodium

The Casserole Queens'
Queso Flameado

Total time 30 minutes

12 oz. fresh chorizo (Mexican sausage), casings removed
1 Tbsp. olive oil
1 poblano pepper, seeded and thinly sliced
½ large white onion, thinly sliced

2 cloves garlic, finely chopped
1 jalapeño, seeded and finely chopped
2 Tbsp. tequila reposado (optional)
Kosher salt and pepper

8 oz. mild melting cheese (such as Monterey Jack, Oaxaca, or a combination), shredded
Warmed tortillas, for serving

1 Heat the oven to 350°F. Cook the chorizo in a large skillet over medium heat, breaking it up with a spoon, until beginning to brown, 5 to 6 minutes; transfer to a bowl.

2 Wipe out the skillet and heat the oil over medium heat. Add the poblano and onion and cook, stirring occasionally, for 5 minutes. Add the garlic and jalapeño and cook, stirring occasionally, until the vegetables are just tender, 1 to 2 minutes more.

3 Stir in the tequila (if using) and ¼ teaspoon each salt and pepper; cook until the tequila is absorbed. Transfer half the poblano mixture to a plate.

4 Return the chorizo to the skillet and toss to combine; transfer to a shallow 2-cup baking dish. Top with the cheese, then the reserved poblano mixture, and bake until bubbling up around the edges, 10 to 12 minutes. Serve with warm tortillas, if desired.

Each serving About 310 calories, 18g protein, 4g carbohydrate, 25g total fat (11g saturated), 0.5g fiber, 72mg cholesterol, 690mg sodium

"The oozy, gooey deliciousness of *queso flameado* is as Texan as Friday night football. This dish is traditionally served flambé—but the idea of pouring tequila on top and setting it on fire is a little scary, so we added the liquor to the mixture to get the flavor without the flames."

—Crystal and Sandy

Aarón Sánchez's Chorizo Meatballs

Total time 1 hour

Makes 30 meatballs

1 **lb. lean ground beef**	2 **Tbsp. red wine vinegar**
1 **lb. Cacique pork chorizo**	2 **Tbsp. lard**
1 **egg**	2 **Tbsp. flour**
½ **c. masa harina mixed with**	6 **c. chicken stock**
¼ c. water	1 **bunch scallions, finely**
1 **tsp. salt**	**chopped**
½ **tsp. pepper**	

- 1   **Anaheim chile, roasted, peeled, seeded, and chopped**
- 1   **c. chopped ripe tomatoes**
- ¼   **c. tomato sauce**
- 4   **garlic cloves, minced**
- ¼   **c. chopped mint**
- ¼   **c. chopped cilantro**

1   Mix beef, chorizo, egg, masa harina, salt, pepper, and vinegar in a bowl. Knead the ingredients and make meatballs the size of ping-pong balls. Set aside.

2   In a large wide pot, melt lard and add the flour; brown lightly to make a roux. Add the chicken stock, scallions, chile, chopped tomatoes, tomato sauce, and garlic. Bring to a boil and simmer for 15 minutes.

3   While the broth is simmering, drop each meatball into the broth and cook for 30 minutes.

4   Serve with mint and cilantro.

Each serving (3 meatballs) About 379 calories, 23g protein, 10g carbohydrate, 25g total fat (9g saturated), 1g fiber, 90mg cholesterol, 836mg sodium

Baja Salad (page 57)

Salads & Soups

Whether served before dinner or as their own main-course attraction, these crispy, crunchy salads (like Curtis Stone's Baja Salad) and savory, soothing soups (try Donna Hay's Roasted Butternut Squash Soup!) are sure to please every palate.

Julie Morris' Roasted Vegetable Salad with Black Pepper Vinaigrette

Total time 35 minutes plus cooling   **Makes 4 servings**

2	Tbsp. coconut oil
½	lb. purple potatoes (or fingerling or small red potatoes), quartered and cut into ½-in.-thick slices
1 to 2 cloves garlic, minced	
1	sprig rosemary, cut in half
2	medium zucchinis, cut into ½-in. cubes
½	medium eggplant, peeled and cut into ½-in. cubes
8 to 12 c. mixed baby greens	

Black Pepper Balsamic Vinaigrette
Sea salt and freshly cracked black pepper

1   Roast the vegetables first: Preheat the oven to 400°F, with a large roasting pan inside. Once the pan is hot, remove it from the oven and spread the coconut oil across the bottom. Toss together the potatoes, garlic, and rosemary in the pan, dressing well with the oil. Spread into a single, flat layer and put in the oven for 10 minutes. Remove the pan from the oven and add the zucchini, tossing to combine, then spread back into an even layer. Return the pan to the oven for another 5 minutes. Add the eggplant, season with salt and pepper, and toss again before finishing the roasting for 15 minutes more. Once fully cooked, let the roasted vegetables cool to room temperature before assembling the salad. Remove and discard the rosemary sprigs.

2   To serve, gently toss the baby greens with half of the Black Pepper Balsamic Vinaigrette in a large bowl, and arrange on serving plates. Top with a generous mound of roasted vegetables and drizzle the plate with a little additional dressing.

Each serving About 249 calories, 4g protein, 24g carbohydrate, 17g total fat (7g saturated), 6g fiber, 0mg cholesterol, 340mg sodium

Black Pepper Balsamic Vinaigrette

Mix together **2 Tbsp. balsamic vinaigrette, 2 Tbsp. EFA oil, ¼ c. apple juice, 1 Tbsp. freshly cracked black pepper, ¼ tsp. garlic powder, 1 tsp. Dijon mustard**, and **1 tsp. kelp powder**. Makes slightly more than ½ cup.

John Besh's
Sugar Snap Pea Salad with Pecans

Total time 25 minutes

Makes 8 servings

½ c. pecan halves
2 Tbsp. olive oil
Salt
1 lb. sugar snap peas, ends
   snapped, strings removed,
   and thinly sliced on the bias

Vinaigrette
¾ c. olive oil
¼ c. balsamic vinegar
1 clove garlic, minced
Leaves from 1 sprig fresh basil,
   minced

Salt and freshly ground black
   pepper

1 Preheat the oven to 325°F. In a small bowl, drizzle the pecans with the olive oil and salt and toss to coat well. Scatter the pecans in a single layer on a baking sheet and bake for 15 minutes, or until golden brown and fragrant. Cool and reserve.

2 Bring a large pot of water to boil over medium heat. Just before you're ready to serve, add the peas and cook for just 1 minute. With a slotted spoon, transfer the peas to a big bowl of ice water to stop the cooking and hold their color. Drain and place in a serving bowl.

3 For the vinaigrette, whisk together the olive oil, vinegar, garlic, and basil in a small bowl. Season with salt and pepper. Pour the vinaigrette over the peas and toss to coat. Sprinkle the toasted pecans over the top.

Each serving About 282 calories, 2g protein, 7g carbohydrate, 28g total fat (4g saturated), 2g fiber, 0mg cholesterol, 86mg sodium

Bobby Flay's Avocado Salad with Lime and Cumin Vinaigrette

Total time 25 minutes

1   Tbsp. cumin seeds
¼   c. fresh lime juice
    (from about 2 limes)
¼   c. chopped fresh cilantro
    leaves, plus ½ c. whole leaves
2   Tbsp. rice vinegar
1   Tbsp. honey

Kosher salt and freshly ground
    black pepper
¼   c. olive oil
¼   c. vegetable oil
4   c. arugula leaves (about 6 oz.)
2   lb. large ripe tomatoes, cut
    into 1-in. chunks, or cherry
    tomatoes cut into halves

4   large ripe Hass avocados,
    halved, pitted, peeled, and
    cut into 1-in. chunks
1   large red onion, thinly sliced
1   tsp. ground cumin

1   In 10-inch skillet, toast cumin seeds on medium-low for 3 to 5 minutes, or until fragrant. Remove from heat; let cool completely.

2   In medium bowl, whisk together lime juice, chopped cilantro leaves, vinegar, honey, toasted cumin seeds, 1 teaspoon salt, and ¼ teaspoon pepper. Add oils in slow, steady stream, whisking to combine. Dressing can be transferred to airtight container and refrigerated for up to 3 hours.

3   Arrange arugula on serving platter. Top with tomatoes, avocados, and red onion. Drizzle with half of vinaigrette. Sprinkle with ground cumin and cilantro leaves. Serve with additional vinaigrette on the side, if desired.

Each serving About 245 calories, 4g protein, 16g carbohydrate, 21g total fat (3g saturated), 8g fiber, 0mg cholesterol, 140mg sodium

Joy Bauer's
Vinaigrettes and Dressings

A salad isn't complete without its drizzle of dressing. Here are 3 different dressing and vinaigrette recipes from Joy Bauer that promise to add flavor and the perfect finish to any salad.

Thousand Islands Dressing

Combine **3 tablespoons reduced-fat mayonnaise, 2 tablespoons ketchup, ½ teaspoon Worcestershire sauce, 1 tablespoon pickle relish,** and **½ teaspoon horseradish** (optional) and whisk together. Dressing will keep for up to one week in fridge in airtight container. Makes 3 servings (2 tablespoons each).

Light Caesar Dressing

Add **¾ cup low-fat buttermilk; 1 clove garlic,** minced (or **¼ teaspoon garlic powder); ½ cup grated Parmesan cheese; 1 anchovy fillet** (optional); **2 tablespoons cider vinegar; 1 teaspoon coarsely ground black pepper;** and **salt** to taste, together in a blender or food processor and puree until smooth. Refrigerate for 30 minutes before serving. Dressing will keep for up to one week in fridge in airtight container. Makes 9 servings (2 tablespoons each).

Buttermilk Ranch Dip

Combine **1 cup nonfat sour cream; ¼ cup reduced-fat mayonnaise; ¼ cup nonfat or low-fat buttermilk** (shake well before measuring); **juice of ½ lemon; ½ teaspoon kosher salt; ¾ teaspoon black pepper; 1½ teaspoons onion powder; ½ teaspoon garlic powder; 2 scallions** (white and green parts only), thinly sliced; and **2 tablespoons finely chopped fresh parsley** in a medium mixing bowl and stir well. Makes 16 servings (2 tablespoons each).

"Salads are a nutritious choice as long as you don't overdo it on the dressing! Be sure to keep portions to 150-calories worth of dressing (about 1½ tablespoons of the regular kind) for an entrée salad and 1 tablespoon for a side salad."

—Joy Bauer

Katie Lee's Grilled Sweet Potato and Arugula Salad

Total time 20 minutes

Makes 4–6 servings

- 1 lb. sweet potatoes, peeled and thinly sliced
- 1 Tbsp. olive oil
- Salt and pepper

- 4 c. baby arugula
- ½ red onion, thinly sliced
- 2 Tbsp. chopped mint leaves
- ½ c. mayonnaise

- 1 garlic clove, minced
- 1 Tbsp. Dijon mustard
- 1 Tbsp. white-wine vinegar

1 Preheat a grill or heat a grill pan over medium heat. Brush each side of the sweet-potato slices with olive oil. Grill sweet potatoes 5 to 6 minutes on each side, until tender. Remove from heat and let cool. Season with salt and pepper. Toss sweet potatoes with arugula, onion, and mint.

2 For the dressing, whisk together mayonnaise, garlic, Dijon, and vinegar. Season with salt and pepper, to taste. Refrigerate until ready to serve. Drizzle salad with dressing just before serving.

Each serving About 233 calories, 2g protein, 15g carbohydrate, 19g total fat (3g saturated), 3g fiber, 8mg cholesterol, 342mg sodium

Curtis Stone's Baja Salad

Total time 30 minutes plus onion pickling   Makes 6 servings

Cilantro dressing
- ¼ c. packed fresh cilantro leaves
- 1 clove garlic
- 2 Tbsp. fresh lime juice
- 2 Tbsp. liquid from Pickled Red Onions
- ¼ c. olive oil
- Kosher salt

Salad
- 3 c. coarsely torn romaine lettuce heart (from 1 head)
- 1½ c. very thinly sliced green cabbage
- 4 radishes, cut into matchstick-size strips
- 1 carrot, cut into matchstick-size strips
- 1 c. cherry tomatoes, halved

Pickled Red Onions
- 2 small avocados, cut into large chunks (about 2 c.)
- ½ c. coarsely crumbled Cotija or feta cheese
- 3 Tbsp. toasted shelled pumpkin seeds (pepitas)
- About 1½ c. tortilla chips, coarsely crumbled

1 Make Dressing: In small food processor, process cilantro, garlic, lime juice, and pickled-onion liquid until garlic is minced and cilantro is finely chopped. With machine running, slowly pour in oil until dressing is well blended. Season with kosher salt. (Dressing can be made up to 1 day ahead; cover and refrigerate.)

2 Make Salad: Just before serving, in large wide bowl or on platter, gently toss romaine, cabbage, radishes, carrot, and tomatoes with enough dressing to coat. Season with salt. Drain pickled onions and scatter over salad. Top with diced avocados, Cotija cheese, pumpkin seeds, and crumbled tortilla chips. Serve immediately.

Each serving About 235 calories, 6g protein, 16g carbohydrate, 18g total fat (4g saturated), 6g fiber, 10mg cholesterol, 340mg sodium

Pickled Red Onions

If using boiling onions: In medium bowl, stir **⅓ c. fresh lime juice**, **¼ c. distilled white vinegar**, and **1 tsp. kosher salt** together. Heat medium saucepan of water to boiling on high. Add **10 oz. small red boiling onions** (about 30), peeled and halved; boil 1 minute or until just softened. With slotted spoon, transfer to bowl with lime juice mixture. Cover and refrigerate, stirring occasionally, at least 40 minutes or until cold. Makes 2 cups.

If using sliced onions: In small bowl, combine **1 red onion, thinly sliced (about 1 c.)**; **⅓ c. fresh lime juice**; **¼ c. distilled white vinegar**; and **1 tsp. kosher salt**. Cover; refrigerate at least 20 minutes, stirring occasionally. Makes ¾ cup.

Transfer to a jar; refrigerate (up to 2 weeks) until ready to use.

Daphne Oz's Cinnamon-Spiced Sweet Potato Soup with Maple Croutons

Total time 35 minutes

Makes 4 servings

4 Tbsp. olive oil
1 lb. carrots (about 4 large), cut into ½-in. pieces
1 large onion, chopped
2 cloves garlic, finely chopped
1 tsp. ground cinnamon

¼ tsp. cayenne pepper
Pinch nutmeg
1 lb. sweet potatoes (about 2 medium), peeled and cut into ¾-in. pieces

2 Tbsp. chicken or vegetable bouillon base
2 dried bay leaves
2 slices leftover bread, cut or torn into 1-in. pieces
1 Tbsp. maple syrup

1 Heat 2 tablespoons oil in a large saucepan over medium heat. Add the carrots, onion, and garlic and cook, stirring occasionally, until the vegetables are starting to brown at the edges, 8 to 10 minutes. Add the spices and cook, stirring, for 1 minute.

2 Add the sweet potatoes, bouillon base, bay leaves, and 6 cups water and bring to a boil. Reduce heat and simmer until the vegetables are very tender, 10 to 12 minutes.

3 Meanwhile, heat the remaining 2 tablespoons oil in a large skillet over medium heat. Add the bread and cook, tossing occasionally, until golden brown. Remove from heat, drizzle the maple syrup over the top, and toss to coat.

4 Discard the bay leaves. Using an immersion blender (or standard blender in two batches), purée the soup until smooth. Serve with the maple croutons.

Each serving About 300 calories, 3g protein, 40g carbohydrate, 14g total fat (2g saturated), 6g fiber, 0mg cholesterol, 1,271mg sodium

"This soup is a no-brainer when you need to get something on the table fast. It's easy, has tons of vitamin A (great for eye health!), and is loaded with energy-packed complex carbohydrates, belly-filling fiber, and, of course, so much flavor! Delicious, healthy, and inexpensive? Perfect!"

–Daphne Oz

Rocco DiSpirito's Lobster Bisque

Total time 1 hour 30 minutes

Makes 4 servings

2 (1- to 1¼-lb.) lobsters, steamed by your fishmonger
Butter-flavored nonstick cooking spray
2 medium onions, diced
3 garlic cloves, roughly chopped

1½ tsp. sweet paprika
½ c. sweet white wine, such as Riesling
1 (14.5-oz.) can diced tomatoes in juice
1¾ c. low-fat, low-sodium chicken broth

2¼ c. skim milk
1 Tbsp. cornstarch
Juice of ½ lemon
Few dashes Tabasco sauce
Salt and freshly ground black pepper
3 Tbsp. chopped fresh chives

1 Heat a Dutch oven over medium-high heat.

2 While the Dutch oven is heating, break down the lobsters. Remove the claws and place them in a bowl. Twist the heads off the tails. Add the tails to the bowl, and refrigerate. Pull the outer shell of the head off each body; discard the outer shells. Remove and discard the lung sacs, leaving the tomalley (the soft green paste). Finely chop the bodies with a cleaver.

3 When the Dutch oven is hot, spray it with cooking spray. Add the chopped lobster and cook, stirring occasionally, until most of the moisture has evaporated, about 4 minutes. Add the onions, garlic, and paprika and cook, stirring occasionally, until the onions and garlic are fragrant, about 2 minutes. (It is important not to burn the bottom of the pot, so if mixture begins to brown, reduce the heat.)

4 Add the wine and cook until it has reduced by about one-third, about 3 minutes. Add the tomatoes and their juice. Reduce slightly, about 2 minutes. Add the chicken broth and 1¾ cups of the milk; bring to a boil. Reduce the heat to medium-low and cook at a steady simmer, uncovered, for 20 minutes; the liquid should reduce by about half. Let the stock cool for a few minutes.

5 While the stock is simmering, remove the claw and tail lobster meat from the shells, working on a rimmed baking sheet to reserve any juice. Add the juice to the simmering stock. Roughly chop the lobster meat (there should be about 1¼ cups), and set it aside.

6 Pour half of the slightly cooled stock into a blender. Blend with the shells (yes, the shells!) carefully on the lowest speed until it's as smooth as possible. Strain all of the stock through a fine-mesh strainer into a medium saucepan, pressing on the solids to extract as much liquid as possible (you should have about 3 cups). Return the pureed stock back to the pot with the remaining stock. Put the pan over high heat and bring to a boil.

7 Meanwhile, whisk the remaining ½ cup milk into the cornstarch in a small bowl. Whisk the cornstarch mixture into the boiling stock. Return to a boil, whisking constantly. Cook until the stock thickens, about 1 minute.

8 Stir in the reserved lobster meat, and remove from the heat. (The residual heat from the soup will warm the lobster meat.) Season the bisque with the lemon juice, Tabasco, and salt and pepper to taste. Stir in the chives, and serve immediately.

Each serving About 181 calories, 17g protein, 22g carbohydrate, 1g total fat (0.4g saturated), 3g fiber, 50mg cholesterol, 813mg sodium

Clinton Kelly's
Slow Cooker White Bean Chicken Chili

Total time 5 hours 25 minutes on high or 7 hours 25 minutes on low

Makes 6 servings

2 Tbsp. all-purpose flour
1 tsp. ground cumin
1 tsp. dried oregano
Kosher salt and pepper
1 lb. boneless skinless chicken thighs
2 Tbsp. olive oil

1 small onion, chopped
1 large poblano pepper, cut into ¼-in. pieces
3 cloves garlic, finely chopped
2 (15-oz.) cans cannellini beans, rinsed

2 c. low-sodium chicken broth, plus more if necessary
1 (14.5-oz.) can diced tomatoes
1 (10-oz.) bag frozen corn
Shredded cheese, sour cream, chopped cilantro, and lime wedges, for serving

1 In a medium bowl, combine the flour, cumin, oregano, and ½ teaspoon each salt and pepper. Add the chicken and toss to coat.

2 Heat the oil in a large skillet over medium-high heat. Add the chicken and cook until browned, 2 to 3 minutes per side; transfer to a 5- to 6-quart slow cooker.

3 Reduce the heat to medium and add the onion and poblano to the skillet; cook, stirring, for 2 minutes. Stir in the garlic and cook for 1 minute. Add the onion mixture to the slow cooker.

4 In a small bowl, using a fork, mash together ½ cup beans and 2 tablespoons chicken broth. Add the mashed beans to the slow cooker along with the tomatoes (and their juices), corn, and remaining beans and chicken broth.

5 Cook until the chicken is tender and shreds easily with a fork, 4 to 5 hours on high or 6 to 7 hours on low. If the chili seems thick, stir in additional chicken broth (¼ cup at a time). Serve with shredded cheese, sour cream, cilantro, and lime wedges, if desired.

Each serving About 335 calories, 25g protein, 42g carbohydrate, 7.5g total fat (2g saturated), 13g fiber, 70mg cholesterol, 549mg sodium

Donna Hay's
Roasted Butternut Squash Soup

Total time 1 hour 35 minutes

Makes 4 servings

4½ lb. butternut squash (about 2 medium), halved and seeds removed
1 yellow onion, halved

1 head garlic, cloves separated
Olive oil, for drizzling
½ c. light cream
1 tsp. ground nutmeg

Sea salt and cracked black pepper

1 Heat oven to 400°F. Place the butternut squash, cut-side up, on a baking tray with onion and garlic, and drizzle with olive oil. Roast 50 to 55 minutes, or until squash is golden and cooked through.

2 Scoop squash and onion from their skins and place in a food processor. Squeeze garlic cloves from their skins and add to processor. Add 1 cup water and process until smooth. Transfer mixture to a saucepan over medium heat. Add 2 cups water, cream, nutmeg, and salt and pepper to taste, and cook until soup is heated through.

Each serving About 335 calories, 6g protein, 56g carbohydrate, 13g total fat (5g saturated), 9g fiber, 20mg cholesterol, 152mg sodium

Chef Secrets

Even all-star chefs have sneaky cooking secrets that can shave time and stress from meal prep. They're fessin' up and sharing some of their favorite hacks with you, so go ahead and give them a try!

What in your pantry would shock us?

"My Jack LaLanne juicer. I use it to make carrot-based drinks for my kids."
–Ree Drummond

"Five kinds of anchovies, almond milk, and beef jerky."
–Mario Batali

"Tang."
–David Burke, owner of five restaurants in New York City, Chicago, New Jersey, and Connecticut

How would you doctor up a frozen pizza?

"I'd drizzle a little olive oil on it, then, once it's blistered in the oven, I'd drape it with thin slices of prosciutto crudo and scatter arugula and toasted pine nuts on top."
–Nigella Lawson, author of *Simply Nigella*

"Potato chips or freshly grated cheese and crisp bacon are great additions."
–David Burke

"Crumbled goat cheese, caramelized onions, and jarred pesto— then some olive oil drizzled on top."
–Ree Drummond

"With thin-sliced Spanish chorizo, olive oil, and black olives."
–John Besh

What's your quickie pasta dish?

"Very simple: penne with butter and Parmesan cheese."
–Scott Conant

"Angel hair sautéed with garlic, lemon, chopped ham, and poppy seeds."
–David Burke

"Add angel hair pasta to rolling boiling water for 3 to 4 minutes. Sauté some thinly sliced chile and garlic and throw in some prawns. After a minute or so, add white wine, chopped tomatoes, and spring onions. Add the pasta and toss."
–Gordon Ramsay

"Spaghetti cacio e pepe: I cook pasta, drain it, then put it back in the hot, dry pan with grated pecorino and coarsely ground pepper, and toss it with a little of the pasta cooking liquid."
–Nigella Lawson

What frozen or jarred ingredient saves you tons of time?

"Frozen peas are packed with flavor and add color and texture to almost any dish. And they hardly need any cooking time."
–Gordon Ramsay

"Garlic-infused oil. Nearly every time I cook, I start by dribbling this aromatic stuff in a skillet or Dutch oven. It packs instant flavor."
–Nigella Lawson

"I always have some peeled frozen gulf shrimp that are perfect for a quick sauté served over rice in a tortilla."
–John Besh

"Jarred pesto. A few tablespoons inject huge flavor into soups, pasta, and even quiche filling."
–Ree Drummond

Spaghetti with Tomato Sauce (page 74)

Vegetable & Grain Mains

These delicious and satisfying vegetable and pasta recipes are perfect as hearty main dishes, including Scott Conant's Spaghetti with Tomato Sauce and The Beekman Boys' Grilled Summer Squash Pizza. The bright, beautiful colors and fresh flavor combinations are sure to impress everyone.

Michael Symon's Corn, Zucchini, and Jalapeño Spaghetti with Parmesan Crumbs

Total time 25 minutes   **Makes 4 servings**

2   slices bread
2   Tbsp. olive oil
¼   c. grated Parmesan cheese
12 oz. spaghetti
Zest and juice of 1 lemon
4   oz. thick-cut smoked bacon
    (about 3 slices), cut into
    ¼-in. pieces

2   small zucchini, cut into
    ½-in. pieces
2   jalapeños, thinly sliced
    (seeded for less heat,
    if desired)
2   cloves garlic, thinly sliced

Kosher salt and pepper
1½ c. frozen or fresh corn
    kernels (thawed, if frozen)
½   c. fresh flat-leaf parsley,
    chopped

1 Heat oven to 400°F. Bring a large pot of water to boil.

2 In a food processor, pulse the bread to form small crumbs. Transfer to a baking sheet, drizzle with 1 tablespoon oil, and toss to combine, then toss with the Parmesan. Roast until the crumbs are golden brown, 8 to 10 minutes.

3 Cook the pasta according to package directions. Reserve ¾ cup cooking liquid, drain the pasta, and return it to the pot. Toss with the lemon zest and juice and ¼ cup reserved pasta water (adding more if the spaghetti seems dry). While the pasta is cooking, cook the bacon in a large skillet over medium heat, stirring occasionally, until crisp, 6 to 8 minutes. Transfer to a paper towel-lined plate.

4 Wipe out the skillet and heat over medium-high heat. Add the remaining tablespoon oil, then the zucchini, and cook, tossing occasionally, until beginning to brown, about 2 minutes. Add the jalapeños, garlic, ½ teaspoon salt, and ¼ teaspoon pepper and cook for 1 minute.

5 Reduce heat to medium, add the corn, and cook until heated through, about 2 minutes. Toss with the pasta. Toss the Parmesan crumbs with the parsley and bacon and serve over the pasta.

Each serving About 526 calories, 18g protein, 84g carbohydrate, 13g total fat (3g saturated), 6g fiber, 8mg cholesterol, 242mg sodium

Mario Batali's
Eggplant Caponata Subs

Total time 1 hour   **Makes 4 subs**

¼ c. extra-virgin olive oil, plus more as needed

2 cloves garlic, halved

1 large Spanish onion, cut into ½-in. dice

2 ribs celery, cut into ¼-in. dice

2 tsp. chopped fresh thyme

2 medium eggplant, cut into ½-in. cubes (about 4 c.)

Kosher salt and freshly ground black pepper

1 (6-oz.) can tomato paste

¼ c. dried currants

¼ c. pine nuts

1 tsp. ground cinnamon

1 tsp. unsweetened cocoa powder

1 Tbsp. red pepper flakes

2 Tbsp. red wine vinegar

2 tsp. sugar

1 baguette, cut into 4 pieces, each split open for stuffing

¼ c. freshly grated Pecorino Romano cheese

¼ lb. provolone, grated

1 Preheat oven to 375°F.

2 In 12- to 14-inch sauté pan, heat oil over medium-high heat until almost smoking. Add garlic, onion, celery, thyme, eggplant, and a couple pinches salt. Stir, reduce heat to medium, and cook 5 to 6 minutes or until eggplant turns golden. If it looks dry, add another tablespoon oil.

3 Add tomato paste, currants, pine nuts, cinnamon, cocoa powder, and red pepper flakes and continue to cook for 3 minutes more.

4 Add vinegar; allow it to evaporate. Add sugar, salt and pepper to taste, and ¼ cup water and cook for 5 minutes more; remove from heat.

5 Place baguette pieces in oven to toast until golden. Remove and stuff each baguette piece with about ½ cup caponata; top with pecorino and provolone. Place stuffed bread on a baking sheet and return to oven. Bake until cheese is melted. Remove and serve immediately.

Each sub About 555 calories, 25g protein, 73g carbohydrate, 19g total fat (8g saturated), 7g fiber, 32mg cholesterol, 1,005mg sodium

Jamie Oliver's
Killer Mac 'n' Cheese

Total time 1 hour 30 minutes   **Makes 8–10 servings**

Sea salt and freshly ground black pepper
3   **Tbsp. butter**
3   **heaping Tbsp. all-purpose flour**
10 **cloves garlic, peeled and thinly sliced**
6   **fresh bay leaves**

1   **qt. reduced-fat (2%) milk**
4   **c. elbow macaroni**
8   **tomatoes**
1½ **c. grated Cheddar cheese**
1   **c. freshly grated Parmesan cheese**
Few sprigs fresh thyme, leaves picked

Couple splashes Worcestershire sauce (optional)
Grating of nutmeg (optional)
3   **big handfuls fresh breadcrumbs**
Olive oil, for drizzling

1   Get a large saucepan of salted water on to boil. Melt the butter in a large ovenproof saucepan, or a Dutch oven, over a low heat, then add the flour and turn the heat up to medium, stirring all the time, until you get a paste—this is your roux. Add all the sliced garlic (don't worry about the amount, because each slice will caramelize like toffee in the roux). Keep cooking and stirring until golden and the garlic is nice and sticky. Add the bay leaves and slowly whisk in the milk a little at a time to ensure you get a nice, smooth sauce. Bring the mixture to a boil, then leave on a low heat to simmer and tick away, stirring occasionally. Preheat your oven to 425°F.

2   Add the pasta to the pan of boiling salted water and cook, following the package instructions. Meanwhile, roughly chop the tomatoes on a board and season them well with salt and pepper. Drain the pasta and add immediately to the sauce. Give it a good stir and take the pan off the heat. Stir in your grated cheese, chopped tomatoes, and some of the thyme leaves. A little Worcestershire sauce added now is nice; so is a little grating or two of nutmeg. Now work on the flavor—taste it and season it until it's hitting the right spot. You want the pasta to be slightly too wet because it will thicken up again in the oven, so add a splash of water if needed.

3   If you've made your sauce in a Dutch oven, leave everything in there; if not, transfer it to a deep earthenware dish. Bake for 30 minutes in the oven, until golden, bubbling, crispy, and delicious.

4 While it's cooking, put your breadcrumbs and remaining thyme into a frying pan with a few drizzles of olive oil over medium heat. Stir and toss the crumbs around until crunchy and golden all over. Remove from the heat and tip into a nice bowl. Serve your macaroni and cheese in the center of the table, with your bowl of crispy breadcrumbs for sprinkling on top, and a lovely green salad.

Each serving About 444 calories, 19g protein, 53g carbohydrate, 18g total fat (9g saturated), 3g fiber, 46mg cholesterol, 515mg sodium

Scott Conant's
Spaghetti with Tomato Sauce

Total time 30 minutes   **Makes 4 servings**

Kosher salt
Tomato Sauce (recipe opposite)
1   lb. fresh or dried spaghetti

½ c. freshly grated Parmigiano-
    Reggiano cheese
2   Tbsp. unsalted butter,
    cut into pieces

16 whole fresh basil leaves,
    cut into chiffonade
Extra-virgin olive oil, for drizzling

1   Bring a large pot of well-salted water to boil.

2   Meanwhile, heat Tomato Sauce in a large sauté pan over medium heat to further concentrate the sauce's flavors.

3   Cook spaghetti until just shy of tender. Reserve some of the pasta cooking water and gently drain spaghetti. Add spaghetti and a little of the pasta cooking water to the pan with the sauce; the starch and salt in that water will help the sauce adhere to the pasta. Give the pan a good shake, increase heat to medium-high, and let pasta finish cooking in sauce. The sauce should coat the pasta and look cohesive, and when you shake the pan, the sauce and pasta should move together.

4   Take the pan off the heat and add the Parmigiano-Reggiano, butter, and basil. Using two wooden spoons (tongs can tear the fresh pasta), toss everything together well.

5   Divide pasta among serving bowls. Finish with a drizzle of olive oil and serve.

Each serving with sauce About 695 calories, 17g protein, 71g carbohydrate, 38g total fat (9g saturated), 6g fiber, 107mg cholesterol, 1,060mg sodium

Tomato Sauce

Total time 50 minutes

Makes about 3 cups

½ c. plus 3 Tbsp. extra-virgin olive oil	1½ tsp. kosher salt
12 plum tomatoes, peeled and seeded, plus any juices from peeling and seeding, strained and reserved (see Note)	10 cloves garlic
	3 sprigs fresh basil (about 24 leaves plus stems)
	1 to 1½ tsp. crushed red pepper flakes

1 In a wide saucepan, heat 3 tablespoons olive oil over medium-high heat. Add tomatoes; be careful, as the oil may spurt. Add salt and cook, stirring occasionally, until tomatoes soften, 2 to 3 minutes. Lower the heat to medium and, using a potato masher, smash the tomatoes, really working the masher to break them up. If the consistency is thick, add reserved tomato juice to the pan. Cook, occasionally mashing and stirring, 20 minutes.

2 Meanwhile, in a small saucepan, heat remaining olive oil over medium heat. Add garlic, basil, and red pepper flakes and cook, stirring occasionally to wilt the basil, until garlic is golden-brown, about 5 minutes. Remove oil from heat and let the ingredients steep, 5 minutes.

3 Strain about half of the oil into the cooked tomatoes. (Strain and reserve the rest; it's a great bread-dipping oil.) Stir to combine. Remove sauce from the heat. Taste and add additional salt, if needed. The sauce may taste spicy on its own, but it gets balanced when used with other ingredients, especially the pasta, butter, and cheese in the spaghetti.

4 The sauce will keep, covered and refrigerated, for 2 days. Reheat gently before serving.

Note: If your tomatoes are not ripe, bright, and juicy, reduce the number of fresh tomatoes to 8 and add 4 whole canned San Marzano® tomatoes.

Julie Morris' Zucchini Fettuccine with Walnuts and Dulse

Total time 25 minutes plus standing

Makes 2–4 servings

8 medium zucchini 1 tsp. sea salt 2 Tbsp. coconut oil	2 c. diced yellow onion (about 1 large onion) ⅔ c. packed dulse strips, torn into 1-inch pieces	½ c. chopped walnuts ¼ c. fresh minced parsley, plus a little extra for garnish

Dulse is a sea vegetable (sometimes referred to as seaweed), and is among the oldest living species on earth. Sea vegetables have been consumed in Asian cultures for thousands of years, but like so many superfoods, are only recently finding their way into mainstream Western cuisine. They are one of nature's top sources of vegetable protein and provide an abundance of beta carotene, chlorophyll, enzymes, amino acids, fiber, and other micronutrients. Dulse comes in both flakes and strips and can be used in sides, snacks, soups, salads and dressings, and entrees. The company Maine Coast Sea Vegetables (seaveg.com) offers an array of raw, certified-organic, and dried sea ingredients that are of premium quality. You can also find dulse at Julie Morris' personal online store (juliemorris.net/shop), or at natural food stores such as Whole Foods or Eden Foods.

1 Using a handheld vegetable peeler, carefully strip the zucchini, layer by layer, into noodle-like ribbons; avoid/discard the center section that holds the watery seeds. Toss the zucchini strips with sea salt and place in a colander. Rest over a large bowl to catch excess moisture, and let stand for 30 minutes.

2 After 30 minutes, wash the zucchini noodles thoroughly with warm water to remove the excess salt, squeeze lightly to remove a little moisture, and let drain thoroughly. Set aside.

3 Heat the coconut oil in a large skillet over medium-high heat. Add the onions and sauté until they have softened and begun to turn translucent, about 5 to 6 minutes. Toss in the dulse, walnuts, and parsley and cook for 2 minutes longer (the dulse will quickly change color as it cooks). Lastly, add the zucchini noodles, tossing everything together, and cook until the zucchini is just warmed through and has turned bright green, about 1 to 2 minutes. Do not overcook. Remove from heat, season with salt and pepper if desired, and toss with remaining parsley to serve.

Each serving About 351 calories, 12g protein, 31g carbohydrate, 24g total fat (10g saturated), 9g fiber, 0mg cholesterol, 193mg sodium

The Beekman Boys'
Grilled Summer Squash Pizza

Total time 30 minutes plus standing

Makes 4 servings

4	medium yellow or golden summer squash (about 6 oz. each), cut crosswise on a deep diagonal into ¼-in.-thick slices	
2	yellow pattypan squash, cut crosswise into ¼-in.-thick slices	
¼	c. extra-virgin olive oil	
3	garlic cloves, smashed and peeled	
	Salt	
¾	lb. homemade or store-bought pizza dough	
6	oz. soft goat cheese	
1	Tbsp. red wine vinegar	
¼	c. small fresh basil leaves	

1 In a large bowl, combine the squash, oil, garlic, and salt to taste, and toss to coat the squash. Let stand for 1 hour. Remove and discard the garlic.

2 Preheat a grill to medium heat. Lightly oil the grill grates. Place the squash on the grill and cook until grill marks appear on one side, about 3 minutes. Turn the squash over and grill until tender, about 2 minutes. Return the squash to the bowl.

3 On a lightly floured work surface, roll the dough out to a 14-inch round. Place the dough on a nonstick (or floured) cookie sheet and slide the dough onto the grill. Cook until grill marks form on the underside, about 5 minutes. Turn the dough over and top with the goat cheese. Top with the squash. Sprinkle the squash with the vinegar and salt to taste. Cook until the cheese has melted, about 3 minutes. Scatter the basil over the top.

Each serving About 472 calories, 15g protein, 44g carbohydrate, 26g total fat (8g saturated), 4g fiber, 20mg cholesterol, 978mg sodium

"Somehow, yellow squash doesn't have the bad rap that zucchini has, perhaps because it doesn't tend to get too unwieldy in size. We like the pattypan variety with scalloped edges because it's sweet, dense, and not so watery."

–The Beekman Boys

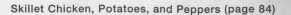

Skillet Chicken, Potatoes, and Peppers (page 84)

Poultry

Poultry is perfect for dressing up or down, depending on your menu's needs. Guy Fieri's California Brick Chicken with Apricot-Mint Chimichurri is perfect for that summer barbeque, while Carla Hall's Buffalo Wing Burgers are ideal for a quick weeknight meal. And think turkey is just for Thanksgiving? Give The Beekman Boys' Maple-Bourbon Roast Turkey a try for your next get-together and banish that notion once and for all.

Sandra Lee's
Mini Chicken Potpies

Total time 1 hour

Makes 12 potpies

½ c. chicken broth
2 cans (10 oz. each) chicken breast, drained
8 oz. frozen mixed vegetables (corn, peas, and carrots)

½ can (10.75 oz.) condensed cream of celery soup
1 Tbsp. garlic-herb seasoning blend
Ground black pepper

5 sheets frozen phyllo dough, thawed
¼ c. (½ stick) butter, melted

1   Preheat oven to 375°F. Line a baking sheet with parchment paper. Arrange 12 oven-safe espresso (demitasse) cups about 2 inches apart on baking sheet; set aside.

2   In a medium saucepan, over medium heat, heat broth. Add chicken and frozen vegetables. Cook, covered, for 15 minutes. Add soup and seasoning blend. Cook and stir for another 5 minutes. Season to taste with pepper. Fill each cup with 1 heaping tablespoon of chicken mixture.

3   Lay out one sheet of phyllo dough (keep remaining phyllo covered with plastic wrap to prevent it from drying out). Brush phyllo with butter. Top with another sheet of phyllo. Brush phyllo with butter. Repeat brushing with butter and layering with 3 more sheets of phyllo (using 5 sheets for one stack). Cut stack in thirds lengthwise. Cut crosswise into fourths. There should be a total of 12 rectangles. Top each cup with a phyllo rectangle and fold corners toward sides of cups.

4   Bake about 25 minutes, or until phyllo turns golden brown and sheets puff up slightly. Serve warm.

Each potpie About 111 calories, 7g protein, 8g carbohydrate, 5g total fat (3g saturated), 1g fiber, 23mg cholesterol, 504mg sodium

"Relax. Have fun with it. Don't get stressed out," says Sandra. "With a little planning, entertaining can be an easy pleasure."

Guy Fieri's California Brick Chicken with Apricot-Mint Chimichurri

Total time 40 minutes plus marinating

Makes 8 servings

1 Tbsp. chipotle chile powder
1 Tbsp. ancho chile powder
2 Tbsp. smoked paprika
2 tsp. ground fennel seeds
2 tsp. garlic powder

1 tsp. dried oregano
1 tsp. sugar
1 Tbsp. kosher salt
1 tsp. freshly ground
   black pepper

2 whole free-range chickens
   (4 to 5 lb. each), butterflied
Apricot-Mint Chimichurri
   (recipe opposite)

1 In bowl, combine chile powders, paprika, fennel, garlic powder, onion powder, oregano, sugar, salt, and pepper. Mix well, then rub all over the chickens, including all gaps in and around joints. Marinate chickens in refrigerator for 1 hour, uncovered (this helps the crust dry out, ensuring a crispy skin).

2 Heat grill to medium; rub down grates with lightly oiled paper towel. Place chickens skin-side down on grill. Watch for flare-ups, as the fat will render and drip; if necessary, move to new spot out of flames. Place foil-wrapped bricks atop chickens.

3 Cook 15 minutes, then remove bricks and flip chickens. Cook 18 to 20 minutes or until temperature between leg and thigh joint reaches 165°F on instant-read thermometer.

4 Transfer chickens to cutting board; let rest for 5 minutes before slicing each into 10 pieces. Serve with Apricot-Mint Chimichurri.

Each serving About 545 calories, 57g protein, 4g carbohydrate, 32g total fat (9g saturated), 2g fiber, 179mg cholesterol, 925mg sodium

Apricot-Mint Chimichurri

Total time 30 minutes   **Makes 2 cups**

½ c. dried apricots	1 tsp. kosher salt
1 tsp. honey	½ tsp. freshly ground black
1¼ c. fresh mint leaves	pepper
¾ c. packed fresh parsley	1 tsp. ground cumin
½ c. packed fresh cilantro	1 tsp. lemon zest
⅔ c. red wine vinegar	Pinch crushed red pepper
4 garlic cloves, peeled	1 to 1¼ c. extra-virgin olive oil

1 Place apricots and honey in bowl; cover with hot water. Soak 10 minutes.

2 Meanwhile, in salted boiling water, blanch herbs 20 seconds. Shock immediately in ice water; spread on a paper towel-lined baking sheet to dry.

3 Remove apricots from hot water; roughly chop. In food processor, combine all ingredients but olive oil; process until finely chopped. With motor running, slowly incorporate oil and pulse until just combined (consistency should be that of a thick sauce). Cover; store in refrigerator to meld, about 10 minutes.

Each ¼-cup serving: About 295 calories, 1g protein, 9g carbohydrate, 28g total fat (4g saturated), 1g fiber, 0mg cholesterol, 250mg sodium

Guy's
Prep-Ahead Tip:
Make 1 day ahead
and press plastic
wrap on surface
(to keep color
from turning)
before storing in
the refrigerator.

Lidia Bastianich's Skillet Chicken, Potatoes, and Peppers

Total time 1 hour 15 minutes

Makes 4 servings

6 slices bacon	1 lb. red bliss potatoes, halved lengthwise	4 small red cherry peppers, seeded and cut into ½-in. pieces
½ c. canola oil	2 Tbsp. olive oil	2 sprigs fresh rosemary
4 small chicken legs, split (4 drumsticks, 4 thighs)	2 small onions, sliced lengthwise 1-in. thick	
Kosher salt		

1 Cut the bacon slices in half crosswise, roll up each piece, and secure with a wooden toothpick. Trim the toothpick.

2 Heat the canola oil in a large skillet over high heat. Season the chicken with ¼ teaspoon salt. Add half the chicken to the skillet, skin-side down, scatter the bacon around the chicken, and cook until the chicken is golden brown and the bacon is crisp, 4 to 6 minutes per side. Transfer the chicken and bacon to a plate. Repeat with the remaining chicken pieces.

3 Wipe out the skillet and return to medium heat. In a medium bowl, toss the potatoes with the olive oil and season with ¼ teaspoon salt. Transfer the potatoes and any oil in the bowl to the skillet. Arrange the potatoes cut-side down and cook until golden brown and crisp, 6 to 8 minutes. Turn and cook on the rounded sides until crisp, about 2 minutes. Add the onions, peppers, and rosemary and toss to combine. Cook, covered, shaking the pan occasionally, for 5 minutes.

4 Return the bacon and chicken (along with any juices) to the pan, nestling it among the vegetables, and cook, covered, shaking the pan occasionally, for 5 minutes.

5 Uncover and cook until any liquid has evaporated, the chicken is cooked through, and the potatoes are tender, about 5 minutes.

Each serving About 565 calories, 42g protein, 24g carbohydrate, 32g total fat (7g saturated), 2g fiber, 197mg cholesterol, 476mg sodium

"My mother taught me to love good ingredients and let produce shine. My grandmother and mother made this dish when we lived in Italy, and now I make it for my grandchildren. It has the flavors of roasted chicken without using the oven."

—Lidia Bastianich

Clinton Kelly's
Crispy Chicken and White Beans

Total time 20 minutes

Makes 4 servings

---

1 Tbsp. olive oil, plus more for
   the pan, if necessary
8 small chicken thighs
1 tsp. dried oregano
Kosher salt and pepper

2 cloves garlic, chopped
4 scallions, chopped (white and
   green parts separated)
2 Tbsp. fresh lemon juice
2 (15-oz.) cans cannellini beans,
   rinsed

½ c. fresh flat-leaf parsley,
   roughly chopped
Pinch freshly grated nutmeg
   (optional)

1 Heat 1 tablespoon oil in a large skillet over medium heat. Season the chicken with the oregano and ½ teaspoon each salt and pepper and cook, skin-side down, until the skin is golden brown and crisp, 7 to 8 minutes.

2 Turn and continue cooking until the chicken is cooked through, 5 to 6 minutes more. Transfer the chicken to plates.

3 Discard all but 1 tablespoon of fat (adding additional oil, if necessary), then add the garlic and the white parts of the scallions and cook, stirring, for 1 minute. Add the lemon juice and ¼ cup water and cook, scraping up any brown bits, for 1 minute.

4 Add the beans, parsley, the green parts of the scallions, nutmeg (if using), and ¼ teaspoon each salt and pepper and cook, tossing, until the beans are just heated through, about 1 minute. Serve with the chicken.

Each serving About 738 calories, 60g protein, 37g carbohydrate, 36g total fat (9g saturated), 17g fiber, 270mg cholesterol, 819mg sodium

The Beekman Boys' Maple-Bourbon Roast Turkey with Gravy

Total time 3 hours 15 minutes   **Makes 12 servings**

1 **(14-lb.) turkey, rinsed and patted dry (neck and giblets reserved)**	1 **orange**	2 **Tbsp. molasses**
¼ **c. coarse salt**	1 **lime**	2 **Tbsp. light brown sugar**
1 **Tbsp. sugar**	1 **small yellow onion, halved**	1 **Tbsp. Worcestershire sauce**
2 **tsp. ancho chile powder**	2 **bay leaves**	2 **c. bourbon**
	3 **garlic cloves, unpeeled**	**Butter, for buttering foil (optional)**
	¾ **c. maple syrup**	⅓ **c. all-purpose flour**

1 Preheat oven to 325°F. Tuck wing tips under turkey by bending them back and pushing them under wings. In a small bowl, combine salt, sugar, and chile powder. Carefully run your fingers under breast and thigh skin to loosen, then rub meat with about one-third of seasoning. Rub remaining seasoning in cavity of turkey and all over skin. Next, pierce orange and lime with a fork, and stuff citrus in cavity, along with onion, bay leaves, and garlic. Using kitchen string, tie legs together.

2   In a small skillet, stir maple syrup, molasses, brown sugar, and Worcestershire sauce. Bring to a simmer; let cook for 5 minutes.

3   Set turkey, breast-side up, in a large roasting pan fitted with a rack. Put turkey neck and giblets in bottom of pan and add bourbon. Pour all but ⅓ cup maple-syrup mixture over turkey. Cover pan with lid or buttered aluminum foil. Roast turkey, covered, for 1 hour 30 minutes.

4   Uncover pan and brush turkey with reserved maple-syrup mixture. Return turkey to oven and continue to roast, uncovered, until an instant-read thermometer inserted into thigh meat registers 165°F, 40 to 50 minutes. Lift turkey from pan, allowing any juices in cavity to drain into pan, and transfer to a platter or cutting board. Tent turkey with foil and let rest, 30 minutes.

5   Discard neck and giblets and pour juices from roasting pan into a gravy separator or large measuring cup. Remove fat, reserving 3 tablespoons. If needed, add enough water to pan juices to measure 4 cups.

6   Place reserved turkey fat in a large saucepan over low heat. Gradually whisk in flour and cook, whisking constantly, until flour has browned, about 5 minutes. Gradually whisk in pan juices and cook, whisking constantly, until gravy is creamy and slightly thickened, about 10 minutes.

Each serving About 745 calories, 85g protein, 23g carbohydrate, 33g total fat (5g saturated), 0g fiber, 250mg cholesterol, 2,151mg sodium

Joy Bauer's Turkey Meatballs

Total time 1 hour 25 minutes   **Makes 4 servings**

2 jars (26 oz. each) marinara sauce	1 Tbsp. dried Italian herb blend (or 2 tsp. dried basil plus 2 tsp. dried oregano)	¼ tsp. crushed red pepper flakes
1 medium onion	¾ tsp. kosher salt	1¼ lb. lean (90%) ground turkey
1 medium carrot	¼ tsp. freshly ground black pepper	2 large egg whites
2 cloves garlic, minced		¼ c. old-fashioned or quick-cooking oats
¾ c. grated Parmesan cheese		

1   Bring marinara sauce to a gentle simmer in a 5-quart saucepan.

2   In a large mixing bowl, stir together the onion, carrot, garlic, Parmesan, Italian seasoning, salt, pepper, and pepper flakes. Add the ground turkey, egg whites, and oats. Mix thoroughly until the ingredients are well combined.

3   Shape the meat mixture into approximately 20 meatballs, about 1½ inches in diameter. Carefully place all the meatballs in the marinara sauce. Do not stir; stirring will cause the meatballs to break apart. Don't worry if some of the meatballs are not completely submerged in the sauce. Cover the pot and simmer gently for 20 minutes.

4   Remove the lid and gently stir the meatballs to thoroughly coat them with the sauce. Simmer, uncovered, for an additional 20 minutes.

Each serving About 74 calories, 7g protein, 5g carbohydrate, 3g total fat (1g saturated), 1g fiber, 19mg cholesterol, 177mg sodium

"My mom makes a mean meatball, and just the smell of them simmering away brings me back to my childhood home in Tappan, New York. My version uses lean ground turkey and egg whites to keep things light, and comes loaded with the classic flavors of Parmesan, onion, and garlic, plus a little minced carrot for extra sweetness and nutrition. Instead of refined white breadcrumbs, I use whole-grain oats as my binder. "

—Joy Bauer

The Casserole Queens' BBQ Sweet Tater and Chicken Enchilada Stack

Total time 1 hour 40 minutes

Makes 6 servings

Roasted Sweet Taters

- 3 sweet potatoes, peeled and cut into 1-in. cubes
- 3 Tbsp. extra-virgin olive oil
- ¼ tsp. cayenne pepper
- 1 tsp. salt
- ½ tsp. freshly ground black pepper

- 1 c. BBQ sauce
- 2 cans red enchilada sauce
- ¾ tsp. cumin
- 3 tsp. olive oil
- 1 small yellow onion, diced
- 3 cloves garlic, minced
- 1 bag fresh baby spinach

- 1 roasted chicken, shredded
- ¼ c. chopped cilantro
- 3 c. corn tortilla chips
- 2 c. shredded Mexican cheese blend

1   Make the Sweet Taters: Preheat oven to 375°F. Lay the sweet potatoes out in a single layer on a sheet pan. Drizzle with the oil and sprinkle with cayenne, salt, and pepper. Toss to coat. Roast for 25 to 30 minutes or until tender.

2   In a large bowl, whisk BBQ sauce, enchilada sauce, and cumin together; set aside.

3   In a large sauté pan over medium-high heat, heat olive oil; add the onions and cook until transparent, about 5 minutes. Add garlic and cook for 1 minute more. Remove from heat and add 1½ cups enchilada sauce, Sweet Taters, spinach, chicken, and ¼ cup cilantro; fold together until chicken is coated with sauce.

4   Place ¼ cup of the remaining BBQ/enchilada sauce in the bottom of a 9" by 13" casserole dish. Top with half of the chicken/ Sweet Tater mixture. Sprinkle with 1 cup crushed tortilla chips and cover with ½ cup cheese and about ¼ cup enchilada sauce; repeat layers once and finish with remaining tortilla chips, sauce, and cheese.

5   Cover with foil and bake at 375°F for 30 to 40 minutes, or until warmed through and cheese is completely melted. Cool a few minutes; garnish with extra cilantro.

Each serving About 626 calories, 29g protein, 59g carbohydrate, 36g total fat (11g saturated), 7g fiber, 82mg cholesterol, 2,237mg sodium

Carla Hall's Buffalo Wing Burgers

Total time 20 minutes

Makes 4 burgers

Spicy Mayo

- ¾ c. light mayonnaise
- 1 Tbsp. fresh lemon juice
- 1 Tbsp. hot sauce
- 2 tsp. honey
- ½ tsp. cayenne pepper

Burgers

- 1 Tbsp. unsalted butter
- 1 tsp. olive oil, plus more for frying
- ⅓ c. minced yellow onion
- Kosher salt and pepper
- 2 cloves garlic, minced
- 2 tsp. hot sauce
- ½ tsp. dried thyme leaves
- ½ tsp. crushed red pepper flakes
- 1¼ lb. coarsely ground chicken
- 4 potato buns, toasted
- Celery and Blue Cheese Slaw

Celery and Blue Cheese Slaw

In a large bowl, toss **4 thinly sliced celery ribs, ½ thinly sliced red onion,** and **½ c. chopped flat-leaf parsley.** Add **1 Tbsp. red wine vinegar, 2 Tbsp. extra-virgin olive oil,** zest of **½ lemon,** and **salt and pepper** to taste; toss. Gently stir in **¼ c. blue cheese.** Makes 4 servings.

1   In a small bowl, stir together the mayonnaise, lemon juice, hot sauce, honey, and cayenne until smooth. Refrigerate until needed.

2   In a small skillet, heat the butter and oil over medium-high heat. When the butter is almost melted, add the onion and ½ teaspoon salt. Cook, stirring occasionally, for 2 minutes, then stir in the garlic. When the onion is golden and tender, stir in the hot sauce, thyme, red pepper flakes, and ½ teaspoon pepper. Transfer to a large bowl and cool to room temperature.

3   Gently combine the ground chicken with the cooled onion mixture using slightly damp hands. (Don't overwork it!) Form the mixture into 4 burgers, ½-inch larger in diameter than the buns. Use your thumb to dimple the center of each patty, which helps it retain its flat middle.

4   Heat oil in a large nonstick skillet over medium-high heat. Add the burgers and cook until browned, about 3 minutes. Carefully flip them and cook until the other side is browned and the meat is cooked through, about 3 minutes more.

5   Slather the spicy mayo on each bottom bun, place the burgers on top, cover with the slaw, sandwich with the top bun, and serve immediately.

Per burger About 626 calories, 34g protein, 41g carbohydrate, 38g total fat (10g saturated), 3g fiber, 136mg cholesterol, 1,151mg sodium

St. Louis Ribs with Tequila BBQ Sauce
(page 98)

Meat

However you like your meat—
ground, grilled, seared, rolled in
herbs, or glazed—there's a recipe
here that's sure to become an
instant favorite. Veal is the star
in Tyler Florence's California Osso
Buco with Kumquat-Cranberry
Gremolata, while Gordon
Ramsay's Blue Cheese Burgers
promise the perfect patty. Create
an instant holiday classic with Ree
Drummond's Root Beer-Glazed
Ham and get the kids excited
with Carolyne Roehm's Prosciutto
Pizza. Whatever the meat, these
recipes make it memorable.

John Besh's
Perfect Roast Leg of Lamb

Total time 1 hour 30 minutes

Makes 10–12 servings

1 (6- to 7-lb.) leg of lamb, bone-in	2 Tbsp. olive oil	1 onion, chopped
Salt and freshly ground black pepper	Leaves from 2 sprigs each fresh rosemary, fresh thyme, and fresh marjoram, chopped	2 carrots, peeled and chopped
2 tsp. crushed red pepper		2 garlic cloves, minced
		Zest of 1 lemon

1 Preheat the oven to 450°F. Season the lamb generously with salt, black pepper, and crushed red pepper, then massage the leg with the olive oil and chopped herbs.

2 Scatter the onion, carrots, and garlic in a heavy-bottomed roasting pan. Set the lamb on top of the vegetables. Sprinkle the lemon zest over the lamb.

3 Put the pan in the oven and reduce the temperature to 250°F. Roast the lamb for about 1 hour, until the meat registers an internal temperature of 135°F on a meat thermometer. Strain and reserve both the vegetables and pan juices for the Pan Sauce.

Each serving with sauce About 426 calories, 41g protein, 4g carbohydrate, 26g total fat (10g saturated), 1g fiber, 144mg cholesterol, 468mg sodium

Basic Pan Sauce

In a small saucepan, heat **2 Tbsp. fat from pan juices** over medium-high heat. Stir in **2 Tbsp. flour** and keep stirring for 3 minutes. Add **½ shallot**, minced and stir for a couple of minutes. Stir in **strained vegetables** for a minute more. Add **1 c. chicken or beef broth**, stirring so that no lumps form. Bring to a boil, then reduce the heat to medium-low. Add **1 sprig fresh thyme**, season with **salt** and **freshly ground black pepper**, and let the sauce simmer for a few minutes. Serve with the roast lamb.

"Try to find lamb that is pasture-raised and free of hormones and antibiotics. It makes a great difference – to us and to the lambs! The quality of the meat and being mindful not to overcook it are the secrets to lamb perfection."

—John Besh

Tyler Florence's California Osso Buco with Kumquat-Cranberry Gremolata

Total time 3 hours 15 minutes   **Makes 4–6 servings**

---

1   c. all-purpose flour
Kosher salt and freshly ground
    black pepper
4   **(2-in.) pieces veal shank**
Extra-virgin olive oil
3   **Tbsp. unsalted butter**
1   **onion, diced**
1   **celery stalk, diced**
2   **carrots, peeled and diced**

Zest of 1 lemon, peeled off in fat
    strips with a vegetable peeler
6   **garlic cloves, peeled and**
    smashed
2   **bay leaves**
¼   **c. chopped fresh flat-leaf**
    parsley
1   **bottle California Zinfandel**
2   **c. low-sodium beef broth**

1   **(28-oz.) can whole San**
    Marzano tomatoes, drained

Gremolata
¼   **c. pine nuts**
1   **c. sliced kumquats**
¼   **c. dried cranberries**
2   **garlic cloves, minced**
2   **Tbsp. chopped fresh flat-leaf**
    parsley

1   Put flour on a large plate and season with salt and pepper. Dredge veal shanks in seasoned flour, tapping off excess. Heat a large, heavy pot over medium heat and hit with a three-count of oil. Add butter and swirl around pan to melt. Add veal shanks and sear on all sides, turning carefully with tongs, until they are a rich brown all over. Remove to a plate. Preheat the oven to 375°F.

2   Add onion, celery, carrots, lemon zest, garlic, bay leaves, and parsley to the same pot and cook over medium heat, scraping up browned bits from bottom of pan. Cook vegetables until they start to color and develop a deep, rich aroma, about 15 minutes. Season with salt and pepper. Nestle veal shanks back into pot, add wine, and bring to a boil. Reduce heat and simmer for 20 minutes, or until reduced by half. Add beef broth and tomatoes, crushing with your hands, and stir together. Cover pot, transfer to oven, and braise for two hours, removing lid after 1½ hours. The sauce should be thick and the veal nearly falling off the bone. Discard bay leaves.

3   Make the Gremolata: Toast pine nuts in a small, dry skillet over medium-low heat, shaking pan often, until fragrant and golden, 6 to 8 minutes. Cool pine nuts, then finely chop and place in a mixing bowl. Fold in kumquats, cranberries, garlic, and parsley.

4   Serve osso buco in shallow bowls sprinkled with some of the gremolata.

Each serving About 783 calories, 61g protein, 49g carbohydrate, 39g total fat (14g saturated), 6g fiber, 197mg cholesterol, 887mg sodium

Tyler's Tip:
If you can't find kumquats, "Try my classic gremolata. Omit the kumquats and cranberries, swap in the grated zest of an orange, plus an anchovy fillet—nobody will know if you don't tell them!—and then follow step 4."

Guy Fieri's
St. Louis Ribs with Tequila BBQ Sauce

Total time 4 hours plus overnight marinating

Makes 8 servings

Dry Rub

¼ c. paprika

¼ c. light brown sugar

3 Tbsp. ancho chile powder

3 Tbsp. granulated garlic

2 Tbsp. ground cumin

2 Tbsp. onion powder

2 Tbsp. kosher salt

1 Tbsp. freshly ground
   black pepper

Ribs

2 (3-lb.) slabs St. Louis rib rack

⅓ c. yellow mustard

Tequila BBQ Sauce

Tequila BBQ Sauce

Place **1 California or New Mexico dried chile** in bowl with **¼ c. hot water.** In medium saucepan, combine **1 (6-oz.) can tomato paste; 1 c. light brown sugar; ½ c. white tequila; ¼ c. fresh lime juice; 2 garlic cloves,** minced; and **1 Tbsp. dark molasses.** Stir well and bring to a gentle simmer over low heat. Add chile and soaking water; season with salt and pepper and simmer until flavors meld, 2 to 3 minutes. Process with blender until smooth; set aside. Makes 2 cups.

1 Combine Dry Rub ingredients.

2 Rinse ribs; pat dry with paper towels. Remove thin membranes from bone sides; trim off excess fat. Brush meat with thin layer of mustard; coat heavily with Dry Rub. Refrigerate overnight.

3 Set out 2 large sheets heavy-duty foil. Place 1 rack on each sheet, meat-side down; fold foil over to form sealed pouch. Place pouches on roasting pans; grill over indirect heat on low, 1½ to 2 hours or until almost tender. Open foil; peel back so ribs are exposed. Carefully turn ribs over; cook 1 hour 30 minutes with foil left open. When done, ribs will be tender and meat will have shrunk back from bones.

4 For last 10 minutes, remove ribs from foil and place directly on hot side of grill. Brush with Tequila BBQ Sauce and allow heat to caramelize sauce and crisp exterior. Flip, brush other side, and cook for a final 5 minutes. Serve with additional Tequila BBQ Sauce.

Each serving About 790 calories, 37g protein, 49g carbohydrate, 51g total fat (15g saturated), 5g fiber, 170mg cholesterol, 1,780mg sodium

Jamie Oliver's
Pork Chops with Sage

Total time 1 hour 15 minutes

Makes 4 servings

2	lb. peeled and diced potatoes	2	oz. butter, diced
4	thick pork chops, bone-in	4	dried apricots
24	fresh sage leaves		Sea salt and freshly ground
1	garlic bulb		black pepper
4	slices prosciutto		Extra-virgin olive oil

Flour
6   thick strips pancetta or
     smoked bacon

1   Preheat oven to 425°F.

2   Boil potatoes for 3 to 4 minutes; drain. Lay chops flat, and insert a small paring knife along each chop to make a pocket. Puree 8 sage leaves, 1 peeled garlic clove, prosciutto, butter, apricots, salt, and pepper. Push mixture into each chop.

3   Cover one side of 8 sage leaves with oil, then press into flour. Place two leaves on each chop, flour-side down. Put the pancetta or bacon into a tray with potatoes, remaining sage, and unpeeled cloves. Drizzle with oil and put tray into oven. After 10 minutes, heat olive oil in a frying pan over high heat, and fry chops until golden on both sides. Remove potatoes from oven. Place chops on top, and cook for 10 to 15 minutes more. Remove and serve.

Each serving About 818 calories, 51g protein, 48g carbohydrate, 47g total fat (18g saturated), 4g fiber, 173mg cholesterol, 947mg sodium

Stephanie Izard's Grilled Steak with Stone-Fruit Tapenade

Total time 25 minutes plus marinating and resting   **Makes 4 servings**

Steak

- 3 Tbsp. olive oil
- 1 Tbsp. grainy mustard
- 3 garlic cloves, minced
- 1½ tsp. sambal oelek (chili-garlic paste)
- 4 (1-in. thick) boneless New York strip steaks
- ½ tsp. kosher salt
- ¼ tsp. freshly ground black pepper

Tapenade

- 1½ lb. mixed peaches, nectarines, and plums, pitted and diced
- ¼ c. fresh basil leaves, torn
- ¼ c. niçoise olives, pitted and chopped
- 2 Tbsp. minced shallot
- 2 Tbsp. fresh lemon juice
- 1 Tbsp. extra-virgin olive oil
- ¼ tsp. kosher salt
- 2 to 3 tsp. honey

1 Make steak: Whisk oil, mustard, garlic, and sambal oelek in a small bowl. Pour into a resealable food-storage bag. Add steaks, seal bag, and turn to coat steaks with marinade. Refrigerate 3 to 4 hours.

2 Make tapenade: Combine all ingredients in a medium bowl, adding honey to taste.

3 Remove steaks from marinade and let them sit at room temperature, 30 minutes. Heat a gas grill to medium-high or prepare a medium-high fire in a charcoal grill. Sprinkle steaks on both sides with salt and pepper. Grill steaks 4 to 5 minutes per side until medium-rare, or when a thermometer inserted into meat reaches 135°F. Remove steaks to a platter and cover loosely with foil; let rest 5 minutes. Serve with tapenade.

Each serving About 494 calories, 33g protein, 26g carbohydrate, 29g total fat (9g saturated), 3g fiber, 151mg cholesterol, 587mg sodium

Ree Drummond's
Root Beer-Glazed Ham

Total time 3 hours 25 minutes

Makes 16 servings

½ fully-cooked, bone-in ham (about 7 lb. total, preferably shank end)	40 whole cloves ¼ c. Dijon mustard 2 Tbsp. cider vinegar	¾ c. firmly packed brown sugar Kosher salt and pepper 1 (12-oz.) can root beer

1 Heat the oven to 350°F. Place the ham cut-side down on a rack set in a roasting pan; add ⅓ cup water to the pan.

2 Score the ham on all sides in a diamond pattern, cutting only ¼- to ½-inch deep. Press 1 clove in the middle of each diamond. Cover the ham with foil and bake for 2 hours.

3 Meanwhile, make the glaze: In a medium saucepan, whisk together the mustard, vinegar, sugar, and ¼ teaspoon each salt and pepper. Gradually add the root beer. Simmer, stirring occasionally, until slightly thickened, 15 to 20 minutes. Remove from heat.

4 Brush a third of the glaze (about ⅓ cup) over the ham and bake, uncovered, for 20 minutes; repeat. Brush the remaining glaze over the ham and bake until the ham is heated through and the internal temperature registers 140°F, 15 to 20 minutes more.

Each serving About 259 calories, 26g protein, 14g carbohydrate, 10g total fat (3.5g saturated), 0g fiber, 67mg cholesterol, 1,917mg sodium

"It's so fun to crack open a can of root beer and add it to the glaze. It provides liquid, sweetness, and flavor. Sometimes I use cola or even Dr. Pepper®!"

—Ree Drummond

Ingrid Hoffmann's
Pork-Apricot Fried Rice

Total time 30 minutes

Makes 4 servings

2½ Tbsp. vegetable oil
2 c. long-grain white rice
2 c. unsweetened pineapple
   juice
⅓ c. dried apricots, sliced
Kosher salt and pepper

1½ lb. boneless pork loin,
   cut into ¼-in. pieces
2 cloves garlic, chopped
2 stalks celery, chopped
4 scallions, finely chopped
2 Tbsp. low-sodium soy sauce

2 tsp. sherry vinegar
1 Tbsp. grated fresh ginger
¼ c. fresh cilantro, chopped,
   plus more for serving
¼ c. pistachios, toasted

1 Heat 1 tablespoon oil in a large saucepan over medium heat. Add the rice and cook, stirring, for 2 minutes. Add the pineapple juice, apricots, 2 cups water, and ¼ teaspoon salt and bring to a boil. Reduce heat and simmer, covered, until tender, 15 to 20 minutes.

2 Meanwhile, heat the remaining 1½ tablespoons oil in a large skillet over medium-high heat. Season the pork with ¾ teaspoon salt and ½ teaspoon pepper. In 2 batches, cook the pork, tossing occasionally, until golden brown, 2 to 3 minutes.

3 Return the first batch of pork to the skillet, along with the garlic, celery, scallions, soy sauce, vinegar, ginger, and cilantro. Cook, stirring often, until the celery is tender, 4 minutes. Add the rice and mix to combine. Sprinkle with pistachios and additional cilantro, if desired.

Each serving About 1,020 calories, 44g protein, 109g carbohydrate, 45g total fat (13g saturated), 4g fiber, 102mg cholesterol, 894mg sodium

Gordon Ramsay's
Blue Cheese Burgers

Total time 35 minutes plus chilling

Makes 6–8 burgers

Burgers

- 2 lb. lean ground beef
- 1 small red onion, peeled and minced
- 3½ oz. blue cheese, crumbled
- Small bunch chives, chopped

- Few dashes Tabasco sauce
- 2 tsp. Worcestershire sauce
- 1 tsp. English mustard
- Sea salt and black pepper
- Olive oil, to drizzle

- 6 to 8 soft burger buns, split
- Handful salad leaves
- Sliced tomatoes
- Sliced avocado
- Mayonnaise and/or ketchup

1   To prepare burgers, pull all ingredients, except oil, into a large bowl, seasoning well with salt and pepper. Mix until well combined, using your hands. Break off a small piece of the mixture, shape into a ball, and cook in an oiled pan until cooked, then taste for seasoning. Adjust the seasoning of the uncooked mixture as necessary. Cover the bowl with plastic wrap and chill for a few hours.

2   Preheat a griddle pan or heat up the barbecue. With wet hands, shape the burgers into 6 to 8 neat patties. Brush or drizzle the patties with a little olive oil and cook for about 7 to 10 minutes, turning them over halfway through cooking. They should still be slightly pink in the center.

3   When the burgers are almost ready, drizzle the cut side of the burger buns with a little olive oil. Toast the buns, cut-side down, on the barbecue or griddle until lightly golden.

4   To serve, sandwich the burger patties between the buns with some salad leaves, tomato and avocado slices, and a dollop of mayonnaise and/or ketchup, as you prefer.

Each burger About 472 calories, 33g protein, 24g carbohydrate, 26g total fat (9g saturated), 1g fiber, 89mg cholesterol, 561mg sodium

Katie Lee's Steak Chimichurri with Grilled Tomatoes

Total time 25 minutes plus marinating

Steaks

¼ c. fresh lime juice
¼ c. olive oil
4 garlic cloves, minced
1 tsp. salt
1 tsp. black pepper
2 lb. flank steak

Chimichurri

1 c. cilantro, minced
1 c. flat-leaf parsley, minced
4 garlic cloves, minced
¼ c. red wine vinegar
¼ c. extra-virgin olive oil

1 In a baking dish, whisk lime juice, olive oil, garlic, salt, and pepper. Add steaks and turn to coat both sides. Cover and refrigerate overnight, or for at least 2 hours.

2 Meanwhile, make the chimichurri: Combine the cilantro, parsley, garlic, and vinegar, and then slowly whisk in the olive oil until emulsified.

3 Preheat a grill or grill pan to medium-high heat. Cook steaks to desired degree of doneness, about 4 minutes on each side for medium. Let the meat rest for 10 minutes, then slice thinly and serve with chimichurri.

Each serving About 293 calories, 27g protein, 2g carbohydrate, 19g total fat (5g saturated), 0.5g fiber, 78mg cholesterol, 151mg sodium

Grilled Tomatoes

Preheat grill or grill pan to medium-high heat. Brush **4 ripe beefsteak tomatoes,** cut in half crosswise, with **1 Tbsp. olive oil** on both sides, and season cut sides with **salt** and **pepper**. Place cut-side down on grill, and cook 1 to 2 minutes. Turn, and top tomatoes evenly with **1 Tbsp. fresh thyme leaves** and **¼ c. grated Parmesan cheese;** cook 1 additional minute.

Mario Batali's
Sausage with Lentils and Spinach

Total time 25 minutes plus resting

Makes 4 servings

Kosher salt and black pepper
12 oz. dried lentils
2 cloves garlic, peeled
6 fresh sage leaves

2 medium carrots, peeled, quartered, and thinly sliced
12 oz. sweet Italian sausage
¼ c. plus 1 tsp. olive oil

¼ c. red wine vinegar
½ bunch spinach, thick stems discarded and large leaves roughly chopped

1 Heat oven to 425°F. In a medium saucepan, bring 6 cups water to a boil. Add 1 teaspoon salt, then the lentils, garlic, and sage, and simmer for 15 minutes. Add the carrots and simmer until the lentils are just tender, 3 to 5 minutes more.

2 Meanwhile, place the sausages on a rimmed baking sheet. Prick them with a knife or fork, then toss with 1 teaspoon oil. Roast, shaking the pan once, until just cooked through, 12 to 15 minutes. Transfer to a cutting board and let rest a couple of minutes before slicing.

3 In a medium bowl, whisk together the remaining ¼ cup oil and the red wine vinegar.

4 Discard the garlic and sage leaves from the lentils. Drain the lentils and carrots, and toss with the vinaigrette. Fold in the spinach and then the sausage.

Each serving About 580 calories, 28g protein, 58g carbohydrate, 27g total fat (6g saturated), 15g fiber, 24mg cholesterol, 1,059mg sodium

"If you shop with seasonality and locality in mind, you'll get more for your money (and the best of what's available). Lentils are rich and satiating, and dried lentils can be kept for a long time. This dish will work with almost any protein, so feel free to substitute with whatever's on sale."

–Mario Batali

Carolyne Roehm's Prosciutto Pizza

Total time 20 minutes

Makes 2 pizzas

1 **lb. pizza dough, fresh or frozen**	2 **c. chopped tomatoes**	1 **Tbsp. fresh lemon juice**
4 **tsp. extra-virgin olive oil**	¼ **lb. sliced prosciutto or speck**	3 **c. arugula**
½ **c. grated Parmesan cheese**	½ **tsp. red pepper flakes**	¼ **c. toasted pine nuts**
1 **lb. fresh mozzarella, thinly**	**(optional)**	
sliced	½ **c. oregano leaves**	

1   Preheat oven to 450°F.

2   Oil 2 pizza pans and divide pizza dough into 2 balls. Stretch or roll each one until very thin. Drizzle with 1 teaspoon olive oil and sprinkle with a little Parmesan.

3   Arrange mozzarella and tomatoes on the dough. Add prosciutto, red pepper flakes (if using), and oregano leaves. Bake 12 to 15 minutes.

4   Before serving, drizzle remaining olive oil and lemon juice on arugula, then place on top of pizza. Add remaining grated Parmesan and top with pine nuts, then serve.

Each pizza About 1,612 calories, 76g protein, 112g carbohydrate, 93g total fat (39g saturated), 7g fiber, 252mg cholesterol, 3,586mg sodium

Carla Hall's Poppy-Seed Pork Tenderloin with a Fresh Herb Crust

Total time 30 minutes plus resting

Makes 4 servings

1 Tbsp. canola oil	½ tsp. kosher salt	¼ c. fresh dill, finely chopped
1 tsp. sweet paprika	¼ tsp. freshly ground black pepper	¼ c. fresh flat-leaf parsley leaves, finely chopped
1 tsp. poppy seeds	1 (12- to 14-oz.) pork tenderloin	
½ tsp. ground cinnamon		

1 Heat oven to 425°F. Meanwhile, combine oil, paprika, poppy seeds, cinnamon, salt, and pepper in a small bowl. Rub mixture all over pork and let stand on a rimmed baking sheet at room temperature until oven is heated.

2 Roast pork until it registers 135°F for medium, about 15 to 20 minutes.

3 While pork is roasting, tear a sheet of parchment paper the length of the tenderloin. Sprinkle dill and parsley in an even layer on paper.

4 Roll cooked pork in its pan juices, then transfer to fresh herbs and roll in herbs to coat evenly. Let pork stand 5 minutes, then cut into slices at an angle, and serve.

Each serving About 128 calories, 17g protein, 1g carbohydrate, 6g total fat (1g saturated), 1g fiber, 52mg cholesterol, 284mg sodium

Garlic and Tarragon Shrimp (page 121)

Fish & Seafood

These light and delicious seafood dishes introduce new flavors for your favorite fish. Enjoy Ingrid Hoffmann's Chicharrones Fish Tacos or Donna Hay's Garlic and Tarragon Shrimp—any of these recipes can pull double-duty as family-pleasing weeknight dinners or gorgeous centerpieces at your next party!

John Besh's Trout Almondine

Total time 40 minutes   Makes 6 servings

1 c. milk	6 (5- to 7-oz.) skinless speckled	8 Tbsp. butter
1 c. flour	trout fillets	½ c. sliced almonds
1 tsp. Basic Creole Spices	**Salt**	Juice of 1 lemon
	Freshly ground black pepper	2 Tbsp. minced fresh parsley

1   Pour the milk into a wide dish. Put the flour and Creole Spices into another wide dish and stir to combine. Season the fish fillets with salt and pepper, dip them into the milk, and then dredge them in the seasoned flour.

2   Melt 2 tablespoons of the butter in a large skillet over medium-high heat. Add 3 fillets and cook until golden brown, about 3 minutes per side. Transfer the fish to a platter; cook the remaining fillets the same way.

3   Add the remaining 4 tablespoons butter to the same skillet over medium-high heat. Swirl the skillet over the heat so that the butter melts evenly, and cook until the butter turns brownish, 5 to 7 minutes. Reduce the heat to medium-low, add the almonds, and cook, stirring gently, until the nuts are toasty brown, about 3 minutes. Add the lemon juice, parsley, and a dash of salt.

4   Spoon the browned butter and almonds over the fish and serve.

Each serving About 429 calories, 32g protein, 16g carbohydrate, 26g total fat (12g saturated), 2g fiber, 183mg cholesterol, 808mg sodium

Basic Creole Spices

Mix together **2 Tbsp. celery salt, 1 Tbsp. sweet paprika, 1 Tbsp. coarse sea salt, 1 Tbsp. freshly ground black pepper, 1 Tbsp. garlic powder, 1 Tbsp. onion powder, 2 tsp. cayenne pepper, and ½ tsp. ground allspice** in a bowl. Transfer the spices to a clean container with a tight-fitting lid, cover, and store up to six months. Makes ⅓ cup.

"In traditional French cooking, a whole fish is used for this recipe, but in New Orleans we prefer skinless fillets. Take your time swirling the butter in the pan so that the milk solids brown and give off that signature nutty aroma, and serve the dish while the sauce is still foamy."

—John Besh

Katie Lee's Salmon Cakes with Artichoke Tartar Sauce

Total time 1 hour plus cooling

Makes 8 servings

½ **lb. salmon**	3 **stalks celery, small diced**	1 **clove garlic, minced**
Salt and pepper	1 **red bell pepper, small diced**	1 **c. breadcrumbs**
2 **Tbsp. olive oil**	1 **red onion, small diced**	2 **eggs, lightly beaten**

1 Preheat oven to 350°F. Place salmon skin-side down in a baking dish, and season with salt and pepper. Bake for 15 minutes, until cooked through. Let cool completely. Remove skin, flake with a fork, and put in a medium bowl.

2 Heat 1 tablespoon olive oil in a large skillet over medium heat. Add celery, bell pepper, onion, garlic, parsley, salt, and pepper. Sauté until vegetables are tender, about 10 minutes. Let cool completely, and mix with salmon. Add breadcrumbs and eggs, and mix.

3 Shape salmon mixture (it will be wet) into eight patties and place on a baking sheet. Refrigerate for 30 minutes.

4 Heat 1 tablespoon olive oil in a large skillet over medium heat. Cook salmon patties about 3 minutes on each side. Serve hot or chilled with Artichoke Tartar Sauce.

Each serving (with sauce) About 246 calories, 9g protein, 13g carbohydrate, 17g total fat (3g saturated), 2g fiber, 65mg cholesterol, 371mg sodium

Artichoke Tartar Sauce

In a bowl, mix together **1 jar marinated artichoke hearts,** drained and chopped; **½ c. mayonnaise; 1 Tbsp. capers; 1 Tbsp. lemon juice; 1 tsp. Dijon mustard;** and **salt and pepper** to taste. Refrigerate until ready to serve.

"These are a great money saver—a half pound of salmon goes really far. You'll have leftovers."

—Katie Lee

The Casserole Queens'
Crab, Shrimp, and Goat Cheese Poblanos with Chipotle Sauce

Total time 1 hour   Makes 8 servings

8 poblano chile peppers	1 tsp. ground cumin	½ c. frozen kernel corn, thawed
2 egg whites	1 tsp. freshly ground black pepper	½ c. red bell pepper, diced
8 oz. Monterey Jack cheese, shredded	½ tsp. dried red pepper flakes	⅓ c. chopped fresh cilantro, plus more for garnish
1 (4-oz.) pkg. goat cheese, crumbled	1 (6-oz.) can lump crabmeat, rinsed and drained	3 Tbsp. fresh lime juice
2 Tbsp. shallots, diced	6 oz. cooked shrimp, peeled, deveined, and coarsely chopped	¾ c. plain low-fat yogurt
1 garlic clove, minced		2 tsp. canned chipotle peppers in adobo sauce, finely chopped

"Fairly mild overall, poblano peppers pack a ton of flavor and are perfect for stuffing with a variety of ingredients. In this recipe, we paired the poblano with seafood, which goes perfectly with the mildly spicy peppers and creamy goat cheese filling."

–Crystal and Sandy

1 Turn broiler on high. Spray a 13" by 9" baking dish with cooking spray; set aside. Broil chile peppers on a foil-lined baking sheet, 5 inches from heat source, for 5 minutes on each side or until peppers look blistered. Lower oven temperature to 375°F.

2 Place peppers in a large zip-top plastic bag; seal and let stand 10 minutes to loosen skins. Peel and carefully cut peppers open lengthwise on one side, keeping stems intact; discard seeds. Set peppers aside.

3 Process egg whites in a food processor until foamy. Add Monterey Jack cheese, goat cheese, shallots, garlic, cumin, black pepper, and red pepper flakes; process until blended.

4 Place cheese mixture in a large bowl. Stir in crabmeat, shrimp, corn, red bell pepper, cilantro, and 1 tablespoon lime juice. Spoon crabmeat mixture evenly into peppers, pinching cut edges together to seal. Arrange stuffed peppers, seam-side down, in prepared baking dish.

5 Bake, covered, for 25 to 30 minutes or until thoroughly heated. While peppers bake, combine remaining lime juice, yogurt, and chipotle peppers in a small bowl; set aside. To serve, drizzle sauce over peppers and sprinkle with cilantro.

Each serving About 234 calories, 21g protein, 10g carbohydrate, 13g total fat (8g saturated), 2g fiber, 92mg cholesterol, 436mg sodium

Carolyne Roehm's Seafood Pasta

Total time 40 minutes   Makes 6 servings

1 lb. corn pasta (or any kind of pasta)	Juice and zest of 1 large lemon	Few threads saffron
8 cloves garlic, sliced	Salt and pepper	½ c. fresh oregano leaves
1 large onion, diced	24 clams	¼ tsp. hot pepper flakes
⅓ c. olive oil	2 c. chopped tomatoes	2 lb. shrimp (21 to 25 count), cleaned and deveined
	2 c. fresh or 1 lb. frozen fava beans	

1   Cook pasta until al dente; drain and reserve cooking water.

2   Sauté garlic and onion in olive oil until translucent; add lemon juice and 3 cups of pasta water. Add salt and pepper to taste; cook until cooking water reduces to ½ cup.

3   Add clams and cook until they open, about 3 to 4 minutes. Remove clams from sauce and keep warm. Add tomatoes, fava beans, saffron, oregano leaves, hot pepper flakes, and more pasta water, if necessary, and bring to a boil, 1 minute.

4   Lower heat and add shrimp; cook until shrimp are done.

5   Add clams, pour over pasta, garnish with lemon zest, and serve.

Each serving About 583 calories, 45g protein, 69g carbohydrate, 15g total fat (2g saturated), 12g fiber, 237mg cholesterol, 719mg sodium

Donna Hay's
Garlic and Tarragon Shrimp

Total time 50 minutes   **Makes 4 servings**

1 head garlic, unpeeled
1 Tbsp. olive oil
4 Tbsp. unsalted butter, softened

1 bunch tarragon, chopped
1 tsp. dried chile flakes
Sea salt and cracked black pepper

1 lb. large shrimp (16 to 20 count), butterflied with tails intact

1   Heat oven to 350°F. Place garlic on a baking tray, drizzle with olive oil, and roast 30 minutes. Remove garlic from oven and increase temperature to 425°F.

2   Squeeze garlic cloves from their skins, place in a bowl, and mash until smooth. Add butter, tarragon, chile flakes, and salt and pepper to taste; mix to combine.

3   Place shrimp on a baking tray, top with garlic and butter mixture, and cook 6 to 8 minutes or until cooked through.

Each serving About 230 calories, 17g protein, 4g carbohydrate, 16g total fat (8g saturated), 0.5g fiber, 173mg cholesterol, 766mg sodium

Ingrid Hoffmann's Chicharrones Fish Tacos with Chipotle Tartar Sauce

Total time 1 hour 10 minutes

Makes 4–8 servings

Tartar Sauce

- 2 garlic cloves, finely chopped
- 2 chipotles en adobo, seeded and finely chopped
- ¾ c. mayonnaise
- 1 scallion, white and light green parts, finely chopped
- 1 Tbsp. lime juice
- **Salt, to taste**

Tacos

- 2 lb. skinless red snapper fillets (or other firm, flaky white fish)
- 2 Tbsp. Worcestershire sauce
- 4 garlic cloves, finely minced
- 1 tsp. salt
- ⅛ tsp. freshly ground black pepper
- 1 c. all-purpose flour
- 3 c. vegetable oil, for frying
- 8 (8-in.) flour tortillas
- 1 cucumber, peeled, seeded, and sliced into ½-in.-thick long strips
- 6 oz. arugula leaves
- 1 c. fresh cilantro
- **Zest of 2 oranges**
- **Lime wedges, for serving**

1 For Chipotle Tartar Sauce: Combine all tartar sauce ingredients in small bowl and mix. Salt to taste. Cover with plastic wrap and refrigerate until ready to use.

2 For Fish Tacos: Rinse fish under cold water and pat dry with paper towels. Cut into 1-inch cubes and place in a bowl. Add Worcestershire sauce, garlic, salt, and pepper and turn the fish to coat in the ingredients. Cover with plastic wrap and refrigerate for 20 minutes.

3 Place flour in a shallow dish and toss in fish pieces, a few at a time, until they're all evenly coated.

4 Heat vegetable oil in a large pot over medium-high heat. Fry the fish, a few pieces at a time, in the oil until golden brown, about 4 to 6 minutes. Transfer to a paper towel-lined plate to drain.

5 Warm each tortilla in a hot pan for 10 to 15 seconds on each side. Place on a plate, cover with a kitchen towel, and set aside. Keep warm.

6 Spread a dollop of the Chipotle Tartar Sauce on a warmed tortilla. Add strips of cucumber and top with 3 or 4 pieces of fish. Add a few arugula and cilantro leaves, and a sprinkle of orange zest. Serve with more Chipotle Tartar Sauce and lime wedges on the side.

Each serving About 691 calories, 39g protein, 55g carbohydrate, 34g total fat (6g saturated), 3g fiber, 63mg cholesterol, 1,265mg sodium

Honey-Rum Baked Black Beans (page 130)

Side Dishes

Side dishes are just as important—and should be just as delicious—as the main event! Give your meal a superstar sidekick with Ree Drummond's Herbed Potatoes au Gratin or Curtis Stone's Quick-Braised Spring Vegetables. Turn a veggie mainstay into something special with Guy Fieri's Perfect Grilled Corn—it comes with five different butters and spreads to create the perfect cob.

Curtis Stone's
Quick-Braised Spring Vegetables

Total time 25 minutes

Makes 6 servings

- 1 spring onion or 4 green onions, trimmed and sliced
- 2 cloves garlic, finely chopped
- 3 Tbsp. olive oil
- 3 Tbsp. lower-sodium chicken broth or water
- 8 oz. asparagus, trimmed and cut into ½-in. pieces
- 1 c. shelled fresh fava beans (from about 1 lb. pods), peeled, or sugar snap peas, trimmed and halved crosswise
- 1 c. shelled fresh English peas (from about 1 lb. peas in the pod) or frozen peas (thawed)
- ½ head escarole, torn into bite-size pieces (about 2 c.)
- 3 c. loosely packed baby spinach leaves
- ½ c. loosely packed fresh basil leaves
- 1 Tbsp. finely grated lemon peel
- 1 Tbsp. fresh lemon juice
- 1 Tbsp. finely chopped fresh chives
- Parmesan cheese, for serving

1 In heavy 12-inch skillet, combine spring onion, garlic, oil, and broth; heat to simmering on medium heat. Cover; cook about 2 minutes, or until onion softens slightly.

2 Add asparagus, fava beans, and peas and sauté 2 to 3 minutes, or until beans and peas are heated through. Add escarole, spinach, and basil; sauté 2 to 3 minutes, or until escarole wilts and asparagus is crisp-tender.

3 Stir in lemon peel and juice. Season to taste with kosher salt. Transfer to serving platter; sprinkle with chives and grated Parmesan. Serve immediately.

Each serving About 120 calories, 5g protein, 10g carbohydrate, 4g fat (1g saturated), 4g fiber, 4mg cholesterol, 250mg sodium

John Besh's
Tomatoes with Crabmeat

Total time 30 minutes

Makes 6 servings

6 medium to large ripe Creole
   or other in-season tomatoes
Salt
½ c. mayonnaise

1 sprig fresh basil, 6 small
   leaves reserved for garnish
   and the rest finely chopped
2 Tbsp. fresh lemon juice
1 tsp. Dijon mustard
2 c. jumbo lump crabmeat,
   picked over

Basic Creole Spices (see recipe,
   page 115)
3 to 6 chive or garlic chive
   blossoms, for garnish
   (optional)

1 To peel the tomatoes, bring a medium pot of water to boil over high heat. Core the tomatoes, then score the bottoms by making a small X. Blanch 3 tomatoes at a time for exactly 5 seconds per batch, moving them around with a pair of tongs or a slotted spoon. Transfer the tomatoes cored-side down to paper towels to drain and cool briefly, then peel off skin and discard.

2 Using a teaspoon and starting at the core, carefully scoop out the center of each tomato, creating a bowl. Cut the bottom thirds off and set aside (you'll use them as lids to top the tomatoes). Season tomatoes with a little salt.

3 Mix the mayonnaise, chopped basil, lemon juice, and mustard together in a medium bowl. Add the crab, stirring gently so as not to break up the meat. Season the crab salad with Basic Creole Spices and salt. Stuff the tomatoes with the crab salad and garnish each with a basil leaf and chive blossom, if using. Set a tomato lid on top of each one.

Each serving About 187 calories, 9g protein, 8g carbohydrate, 14g total fat (2g saturated), 1g fiber, 45mg cholesterol, 902mg sodium

Bobby Flay's
Honey-Rum Baked Black Beans

Total time 3 hours plus soaking

Makes 8 side-dish servings

1	lb. dried black beans, picked over
8	oz. dried chorizo, casing removed
1	large Spanish onion (10 to 12 oz.)
2	medium carrots

5	cloves garlic
1	Tbsp. canola oil
1	c. dark rum
⅓	c. clover honey
¼	c. molasses
¼	c. packed light brown sugar

1	can (14 to 14½ oz.) lower-sodium chicken broth (1¾ c.)
1	c. barbecue sauce
⅓	c. plus 2 Tbsp. fresh cilantro leaves, coarsely chopped
	Kosher salt and freshly ground black pepper

1 In large bowl, place beans and add cold water to cover by 2 inches. Soak for 8 hours.

2 Drain beans; place in 8-quart saucepot and add cold water to cover by 2 inches. Heat to boiling on high. Reduce heat to medium, partially cover, and simmer 1 to 1½ hours, or until very tender, stirring occasionally. Drain beans and place in large bowl.

3 Preheat oven to 325°F. Cut chorizo, onion, and carrots into small dice. Finely chop garlic.

4 In 12-inch skillet, heat oil on high. Add chorizo and cook 5 to 7 minutes, or until golden brown and crisp, stirring occasionally. With slotted spoon, transfer to paper towel-lined plate to drain. To fat in pan, add onion and carrots; cook 5 to 6 minutes or until softened, stirring frequently. Add garlic and cook 1 minute, stirring. Add rum and cook 3 minutes, or until reduced by half.

5 Transfer onion mixture to bowl with beans, along with honey, molasses, brown sugar, broth, barbecue sauce, chorizo, and ⅓ cup cilantro. Mix gently to combine, and stir in ½ teaspoon salt and ¼ teaspoon pepper. Transfer mixture to deep 2- to 2½-quart baking dish. Cover tightly with foil.

6 Bake 30 minutes. Uncover and bake 45 minutes longer, or until golden brown on top. Let stand at least 10 minutes before serving. Garnish with remaining 2 tablespoons cilantro.

Each serving About 520 calories, 20g protein, 79g carbohydrate, 13g total fat (2.5g saturated), 15g fiber, 25mg cholesterol, 865mg sodium

Carla Hall's
Sweet Corn and Tomato Relish

Total time 30 minutes   **Makes 4 servings**

- 4 ears corn, husks and silks removed
- 2 Tbsp. extra-virgin olive oil, plus more for grilling corn
- 1 large tomato, peeled, cored, seeded, and finely diced
- ½ small red onion, very finely diced
- 1 jalapeño chile, stemmed, seeded, and finely chopped
- 2 small garlic cloves, finely minced
- Zest and juice of 1 lime
- 1 tsp. ground cumin
- ½ tsp. kosher salt
- 1 Tbsp. fresh cilantro leaves, coarsely chopped

1 Heat grill on high heat until very hot. Rub corn with enough oil to lightly coat. Grill, turning occasionally, until blackened in spots and starting to pop, about 5 minutes. (Don't overcook! Corn should still be yellow and have a bite.) Transfer to plate and let cool.

2 When cool enough to handle, lay each ear of corn on its side and cut off one side of kernels. Rotate cob and cut off another side of kernels. Keep rotating and cutting until all kernels are off.

3 Transfer kernels to large bowl and add tomato, onion, jalapeño, garlic, lime zest and juice, cumin, salt, and 2 tablespoons oil. Toss until well mixed. Garnish with cilantro.

Each serving About 180 calories, 4g protein, 23g carbohydrate, 10g total fat (2g saturated), 3g fiber, 0mg cholesterol, 260mg sodium

Guy Fieri's Perfect Grilled Corn

Total time 40 minutes   **Makes 8 servings**

8 ears corn, with husks

1 Pull husks to stalk end of corn without removing; pull off silks. Return husks to original position; tie with kitchen string.

2 In large saucepot or baking pan, soak corn in 10 cups cold water for 10 minutes. (Soaking corn this way helps keep husks from burning on the grill.)

3 Prepare grill for direct grilling over medium-high heat. Place corn on hot grill grate and cook, uncovered, 15 minutes or until tender, turning occasionally. Peel back husks; spread with toppings (recipes opposite), as desired.

Cilantro-Lime Butter

Pulse **6 tablespoons butter**, softened; **1 tablespoon fresh lime juice; ¼ cup packed cilantro leaves;** and **¼ cup packed parsley leaves** in a food processor. Spread on corn.

Each serving About 165 calories, 4g protein, 19g carbohydrate, 10g total fat (6g saturated), 2g fiber, 23mg cholesterol, 85mg sodium

Horseradish-Cheddar

Stir together **⅓ cup low-fat mayonnaise** and **2 tablespoons drained prepared horseradish.** Spread on corn and then coat with **1 cup shredded Cheddar cheese.**

Each serving About 157 calories, 7g protein, 21g carbohydrate, 7g total fat (3g saturated), 3g fiber, 14mg cholesterol, 208mg sodium

Bruschetta

Stir together **2 medium very-ripe tomatoes**, coarsely grated; **2 tablespoons finely grated Parmesan cheese; 2 tablespoons chopped fresh basil;** and **¼ teaspoon salt**. Spread on corn.

Each serving About 99 calories, 4g protein, 20g carbohydrate, 2g total fat (1g saturated), 2g fiber, 1mg cholesterol, 101mg sodium

Taco-Style

In a microwave-safe bowl, microwave **4 tablespoons butter, 2 teaspoons chili powder, 1 teaspoon ground cumin, ¼ teaspoon garlic powder,** and **¼ teaspoon salt** until melted. Spread on corn.

Each serving About 142 calories, 4g protein, 20g carbohydrate, 7g total fat (4g saturated), 2g fiber, 15mg cholesterol, 142mg sodium

Cheesy Garlic-Bacon

Spread **¾ cup garlic-and-herb spreadable cheese** (about one 5-oz. pkg.), softened, on corn. Coat with **4 strips bacon**, cooked and crumbled, and **¼ cup snipped chives.**

Each serving About 170 calories, 6g protein, 20g carbohydrate, 9g total fat (4g saturated), 2g fiber, 19mg cholesterol, 159mg sodium

The Beekman Boys' Sweet Potatoes with Ancho-Maple Glaze

Total time 30 minutes

Makes 12 servings

4 lb. sweet potatoes, peeled and cut into 2-in. pieces	½ stick unsalted butter	2 tsp. salt
½ c. maple syrup	¼ c. fresh lime juice (about 2 limes)	¼ c. chopped fresh parsley, for garnish
	2 tsp. ancho chile powder	

1   In a large pot fitted with a steamer basket set over boiling water, steam potatoes, covered, until firm-tender, about 10 minutes. Set aside.

2   In a large skillet over medium heat, heat maple syrup, butter, lime juice, chile powder, and salt. When maple mixture starts to bubble, add reserved sweet potatoes. Cook, tossing frequently, until maple mixture is thick and potatoes are cooked through, 7 to 10 minutes. Garnish with parsley.

Each serving About 154 calories, 2g protein, 29g carbohydrate, 4g total fat (2.5g saturated), 3g fiber, 10mg cholesterol, 431mg sodium

Stephanie Izard's Baby Summer Squash with Ricotta and Mint

Total time 16 minutes

Makes 4 servings

1 Tbsp. extra-virgin olive oil	½ tsp. kosher salt	¼ c. mint leaves, torn
2 lb. mixed baby zucchini, yellow squash, and pattypan squash, cut into bite-size cubes	⅛ tsp. freshly ground black pepper	½ c. ricotta cheese
	¼ tsp. crushed red pepper flakes	Whole mint leaves, for garnish

1 Heat a large skillet over medium-high heat. Add oil and swirl to coat skillet. Add squashes, salt, black pepper, and red pepper flakes.

2 Cook 5 to 6 minutes, stirring frequently, until squashes are tender. Remove from heat and stir in torn mint leaves. Transfer squash to a serving dish and top with ricotta. Garnish with mint leaves.

Each serving About 133 calories, 6g protein, 12g carbohydrate, 8g total fat (3g saturated), 3g fiber, 16mg cholesterol, 272mg sodium

Ree Drummond's
Herbed Potatoes au Gratin

Total time 2 hours 15 minutes   **Makes 8 servings**

3   Tbsp. unsalted butter, plus
    more for baking dish
1   medium onion, finely chopped
1   c. whole milk
½   c. heavy cream
Kosher salt and black pepper

8   oz. cream cheese, at room
    temp., cut into pieces
3   oz. Parmesan cheese, grated
    (¾ c.)
¼   c. fresh flat-leaf parsley,
    chopped

1   Tbsp. fresh thyme
3   lb. russet potatoes
    (about 5), peeled and
    chopped into ½-in. pieces
Chopped fresh chives,
    for serving

1   Heat oven to 350°F. Butter a 3-quart shallow baking dish.

2   Melt the butter in a large skillet over medium heat. Add the onion and cook, stirring occasionally, until beginning to soften, about 5 minutes.

3   Add the milk, cream, 1 teaspoon salt, and ½ teaspoon pepper and bring to a bare simmer. Add the cream cheese and cook, stirring, until melted, about 3 minutes; stir in ¼ cup Parmesan. Remove from the heat and stir in the parsley and thyme.

4   Place the potatoes in the prepared baking dish and pour the milk mixture over the top. Sprinkle with the remaining ¼ cup Parmesan and cover tightly with nonstick foil.

5   Place the baking dish on a large rimmed baking sheet and bake for 30 minutes. Uncover and bake until the potatoes are tender and the top is golden brown, 50 to 60 minutes more. Let rest for 15 minutes, then sprinkle with chives before serving, if desired.

Each serving About 380 calories, 10g protein, 33g carbohydrate, 24g total fat (14g saturated), 2g fiber, 76mg cholesterol, 521mg sodium

Lemon Blueberry Layer Cake (page 148)

Desserts

It's time to indulge your sweet tooth! Try your hand at the Casserole Queens' Frozen Banana Yogurt Split, or mix sweet and savory with Marcus Samuelsson's Spiced Apple Pie with Cheddar Crust. Craving chocolate? Gordon Ramsay's indulgent Boston Cream Pie is sure to hit the spot.

Donna Hay's Blueberry, Apple, and Coconut Crumble

Total time 40 minutes

Makes 6 servings

⅓ c. plus ½ c. superfine sugar
⅔ c. shredded coconut
1 stick unsalted butter, melted
1 c. all-purpose flour

1 tsp. vanilla extract
4 Granny Smith apples, peeled and chopped
3 c. blueberries

1 Heat oven to 350°F. Add ⅓ cup sugar, coconut, butter, and flour to a bowl and rub with your fingers until mixture resembles coarse breadcrumbs.

2 Place ½ cup sugar, vanilla, apples, and blueberries in a bowl and mix well to combine. Spoon into a 10-inch baking dish or pie plate. Sprinkle crumble mixture on top and bake 20 to 25 minutes, or until golden.

Each serving About 458 calories, 3g protein, 72g carbohydrate, 20g total fat (13g saturated), 4g fiber, 41mg cholesterol, 30mg sodium

Gordon Ramsay's
Boston Cream Pie

Total time 1 hour 40 minutes plus cooling

Crust

Generous ¾ c. unsalted butter, softened, plus extra for greasing

Scant 3¼ c. all-purpose flour, plus extra for dusting

4 tsp. baking powder

Pinch fine sea salt

1½ c. superfine sugar

2 tsp. vanilla extract

4 large eggs, at room temp. and lightly beaten

Scant 1 c. whole milk

Custard Cream Filling

Generous ¾ c. heavy cream

¼ c. superfine sugar

Pinch fine sea salt

5 Tbsp. whole milk

1 Tbsp. cornstarch

2 large eggs, at room temp.

1 tsp. rum (or vanilla extract)

Chocolate Frosting

3 oz. good-quality semisweet chocolate, chopped

2 Tbsp. butter

¼ c. light cream

½ c. confectioners' sugar

1 tsp. vanilla extract

1 Preheat the oven to 350°F. Line two 9-inch cake pans with removable bases, then butter lightly and dust with flour.

2 Sift the flour, baking powder, and salt together into a large bowl. Beat the butter and sugar together in another large bowl until light and fluffy. Add the vanilla extract, then gradually beat in the eggs. Fold in the flour mixture, alternately with the milk.

3 Divide the batter evenly between the prepared pans and gently level the surface with a spatula. Bake for 20 to 30 minutes, until a skewer inserted into the center comes out clean. Leave in the pans for 5 minutes or so, to cool slightly, then turn the cakes out onto wire racks to cool completely.

4 For the filling, heat the cream in a heavy saucepan over medium heat until bubbles begin to form around the edge of the pan. Immediately add the sugar and salt, stirring until dissolved. Take off the heat. In a bowl, whisk the milk with the cornstarch until smooth, then beat in the eggs. Gradually pour this onto the hot cream mixture in a thin stream, whisking constantly. Stir over low heat until the custard is quite thick and smooth, about 5 minutes. Take off the heat and stir in the rum. Let cool completely, stirring occasionally to prevent a skin from forming.

5 For the frosting, stir the chocolate, butter, and cream in a heavy saucepan over low heat until melted and smooth. Remove from the heat and beat in the confectioners' sugar and vanilla. Let cool, stirring occasionally.

6 To assemble the cake, spread the cooled filling over one of the cakes and place the other cake on top. Pour the chocolate frosting evenly over the top, allowing it to drip slightly down the sides. Cut into slices to serve.

Each serving About 582 calories, 9g protein, 72g carbohydrate, 29g total fat (18g saturated), 2g fiber, 172mg cholesterol, 284mg sodium

Marcus Samuelsson's
Spiced Apple Pie with Cheddar Crust

Total time 6 hours 55 minutes

Makes one 10-inch pie

Crust

- 2 c. all-purpose flour
- 1 c. sharp Cheddar cheese
- ½ tsp. kosher salt
- 1 stick unsalted butter
- 7 Tbsp. ice water

Filling

- 1 c. light brown sugar
- 3 Tbsp. all-purpose flour
- 4 tsp. cornstarch
- 2 Tbsp. ground cinnamon
- ½ tsp. ground ginger
- ½ tsp. ground cardamom
- ½ tsp. salt
- 1 pinch ground cloves
- 6 tart apples
- 1½ lemons
- ¼ c. fresh lemon juice
- 3 Tbsp. cold unsalted butter

1   Make the Crust: In a food processor, pulse the flour with the Cheddar and salt. Add the butter and pulse until the mixture resembles coarse meal, with some pea-size pieces of butter still visible. Sprinkle in the ice water and pulse until the dough starts to come together; you should still see small pieces of butter. Scrape the dough out onto a work surface and pat into a disk. Wrap in plastic and refrigerate until chilled, at least 1 hour or up to 3 days.

2   Make the Filling: Preheat the oven to 400°F. In a bowl, combine the brown sugar with the flour, cornstarch, cinnamon, ginger, cardamom, salt, and cloves. Stir in the apples and the lemon zest and juice.

3   On a lightly floured work surface, roll the dough out to a 16-inch round. Transfer to a 10-inch glass or ceramic pie plate; do not trim the overhang. Mound the filling in the crust and dot with the butter. Fold the overhanging dough over the filling, leaving the apples in the center exposed. Bake the pie for 15 minutes, then cover with a sheet of aluminum foil and reduce the oven temperature to 350°F. Bake for 50 minutes. Remove the foil and bake for 15 to 20 minutes longer, until the filling is bubbling in the center. Transfer the pie to a rack and let cool completely, at least 4 hours.

Each serving About 495 calories, 7g protein, 73g carbohydrate, 21g total fat (13g saturated), 4g fiber, 55mg cholesterol, 341mg sodium

The Casserole Queens'
Frozen Banana Yogurt Split

Total time 40 minutes plus freezing

Makes 10 servings

1 (8-oz.) can crushed pineapple	¼ c. maraschino cherries	¼ c. chocolate syrup,
1 c. plain Greek yogurt	1 lb. fresh strawberries	plus more for serving
5 Tbsp. sugar	1 Tbsp. unsweetened cocoa	3 bananas
1½ c. heavy cream	powder	

1 Line an 8½" by 4½" loaf pan with parchment paper, leaving a 4-inch overhang on the two long sides.

2 In a food processor, purée the pineapple (with the juices), ⅓ cup yogurt, and 2 tablespoons sugar until smooth. Transfer to a large bowl. Add ½ cup heavy cream and, using an electric mixer on high, beat until slightly thickened, 4 minutes. Spread evenly into the prepared pan. Freeze for at least 15 minutes while you prepare the next layer.

"Greek yogurt has a rich and creamy texture, and its tangy flavor gives this dessert the perfect combo of sweet and tart."
—Crystal and Sandy

3   Clean the food processor and purée the cherries, 4 ounces strawberries, ⅓ cup yogurt, and 1 tablespoon sugar until smooth. Transfer to a large bowl. Add ½ cup heavy cream and, using an electric mixer (with clean beaters), beat until thickened (it should be the consistency of lightly whipped cream). Spread evenly over the pineapple layer. Freeze while making the next layer.

4   Using an electric mixer (with clean beaters), beat together the cocoa, chocolate syrup, and remaining ⅓ cup yogurt. Add the remaining ½ cup heavy cream and beat until thickened (the mixture should be the consistency of sour cream).

5   Arrange the bananas lengthwise in the loaf pan on top of the strawberry-cherry mixture, cutting to fit as necessary. Gently push them until they are about two-thirds submerged in the mixture. Spread the chocolate mixture evenly over the bananas and freeze until set, at least 4 hours, and then cover for up to 5 days.

6   Thirty minutes before serving, slice the remaining 12 ounces strawberries. In a medium bowl, toss the strawberries with the remaining 2 tablespoons sugar and let sit, tossing occasionally, for 25 minutes (they should become slightly syrupy).

7   To serve, let the cake stand at room temperature for 5 minutes. Run a knife between the parchment and the edge of the pan to loosen it. Using the overhangs, lift the cake out of the pan and invert onto a platter so that the pineapple layer is on top. Remove the paper, spoon the strawberries and any juices over the top, and then drizzle with additional chocolate syrup, if desired.

Each serving About 265 calories, 3g protein, 30g carbohydrate, 16g total fat (10g saturated), 2g fiber, 53mg cholesterol, 27mg sodium

Ree Drummond's
Lemon Blueberry Layer Cake

Total time 1 hour 20 minutes plus chilling

Makes 12 servings

- 1½ c. all-purpose flour
- 3 Tbsp. cornstarch
- ½ tsp. baking soda
- ¼ tsp. kosher salt
- 1½ c. granulated sugar

- 1½ c. (3 sticks) unsalted butter, at room temp.
- 3 large eggs
- ½ c. sour cream, at room temp.
- 1 tsp. pure vanilla extract

- 8 oz. cream cheese, at room temp.
- 1 lb. confectioners' sugar, sifted
- 1 lemon
- 3 pints fresh blueberries (6 oz. each)

1 Heat oven to 350°F. Spray two 8" by 2" light-colored cake pans with cooking spray, line the bottoms with parchment, and spray.

2 In medium bowl, whisk together flour, cornstarch, baking soda, and salt. Using an electric mixer, beat granulated sugar and ½ cup butter on medium-high until smooth and creamy, 3 minutes. Reduce speed to medium and add eggs, one at a time, mixing well after each. Add sour cream and vanilla; beat until combined. Reduce the mixer speed to low and add flour mixture, beating until incorporated.

3 Divide batter between prepared pans and bake until a wooden pick inserted into the cake comes out clean, 27 to 30 minutes. Let the cakes cool in the pans for 10 minutes, then transfer to wire racks to cool completely.

4 Using an electric mixer, beat cream cheese and remaining 1 cup butter until smooth. Add confectioners' sugar and beat until combined. Using a fine grater, zest the lemon over the bowl and squeeze in 2 tablespoons juice. Beat until combined. Cover and chill for at least 1 hour or up to 1 week.

5 Cut the cakes in half horizontally to create 4 layers. Spread a quarter of icing on one layer (about ¾ cup). Sprinkle with a quarter of the blueberries. Sandwich with another layer of cake; repeat with remaining layers. Spread the top cake with remaining icing and sprinkle with remaining blueberries. Refrigerate at least 2 hours before serving.

"I always leave the sides of this cake unfrosted so you see the beautiful layers. In the summer, I use strawberries instead of blueberries."
—Ree Drummond

Each serving About 645 calories, 5g protein, 86g carbohydrate, 33g total fat (20g saturated), 2g fiber, 133mg cholesterol, 183mg sodium

Bobby Flay's
Peach-Raspberry Crisp

Total time 1 hour 35 minutes

1 lemon
1⅓ c. all-purpose flour
1 tsp. baking powder
3 Tbsp. Demerara or
  brown sugar

½ c. plus 3 Tbsp. granulated
  sugar
10 Tbsp. unsalted butter, melted
6 ripe peaches, peeled
  and halved

1 pt. raspberries
¼ c. cornstarch
⅓ tsp. salt
Whipped cream or ice cream,
  for serving

1 From lemon, grate 1 tablespoon peel; squeeze 3 tablespoons juice. In large bowl, combine flour, baking powder, Demerara sugar, 3 tablespoons granulated sugar, and lemon peel; blend in butter until small and large clumps form. Refrigerate 15 minutes.

2 Preheat oven to 375°F.

3 Cut peaches into ¼-inch-thick slices. In bowl, toss peaches, berries, cornstarch, salt, lemon juice, and ½ cup granulated sugar. Let stand 15 minutes.

4 In 2-quart ceramic baking dish, spread fruit. Top with crumbs. Bake 40 to 50 minutes or until filling is bubbling. Cool 30 minutes. Serve with whipped cream or ice cream.

Each serving (without cream) About 365 calories, 4g protein, 56g carbohydrate, 15g total fat (9g saturated), 4g fiber, 38mg cholesterol, 85mg sodium

Carla Hall's Peach Cobbler

Total time 2 hours plus cooling

Makes 12 servings

All-purpose flour, for rolling
Carla's Crust
8 ripe but firm yellow peaches, peeled, pitted, and cut into ½-in.-thick slices
¼ c. granulated sugar

¼ c. packed light or dark brown sugar
¼ tsp. ground cinnamon
¼ tsp. freshly grated nutmeg
1 tsp. fresh lemon juice
2 tsp. amaretto liqueur

1 Tbsp. cornstarch
Pinch table salt
1 large egg
1 Tbsp. water
1 Tbsp. coarse or granulated sugar

Carla's Crust

Chill bowl and paddle attachment of standing electric mixer until cold. In small bowl, dissolve **1 Tbsp. sugar** and **1 tsp. table salt** in **⅓ c. cold water**; chill until cold.

In chilled mixer bowl, combine **2 c. all-purpose flour** and **2 sticks cold unsalted butter**, cut into ½-inch dice, and toss with hands until butter pieces are well coated. Mix with paddle on low speed until butter forms pea-size pieces; add water mixture all at once, increase speed to medium, and beat just until dough comes together.

Flatten dough into two 1-inch-thick rectangles (for cobbler crusts) or two 1-inch-thick disks (for pies). Wrap dough tightly in plastic wrap and chill until firm, at least 30 minutes or up to 1 day. (You can also freeze dough for up to 3 months; thaw in refrigerator or at room temperature.)

1 Preheat oven to 425°F. Line 2 rimmed baking sheets with parchment paper.

2 Lightly dust work surface and rolling pin with flour; swirl 1 dough rectangle to lightly coat bottom (be sure dough can move while being rolled out). Roll dough rectangle from center out; rotate ¼ turn and roll again. Keep rolling and turning until it forms a 13" by 9" rectangle, lightly flouring surface and top of dough repeatedly (use just enough flour to keep dough from sticking, but don't over-flour). Transfer dough to 1 baking sheet; refrigerate.

3 Repeat rolling out with other piece of dough; place on second baking sheet and bake until golden brown, about 20 minutes. Cool completely on sheet on wire rack. Meanwhile, turn oven down to 375°F.

4 While dough is cooling, make filling: On another rimmed baking sheet or in shallow baking dish, combine peaches, sugars, cinnamon, nutmeg, lemon juice, amaretto, cornstarch, and salt, tossing until well mixed. Roast in oven until fruit releases its juices, about 20 minutes.

5 In small bowl, beat egg with water. Transfer cooled baked crust to shallow 13" by 9" baking dish; spread hot peach filling evenly over it. Top with chilled unbaked dough, brush with egg wash, and sprinkle with coarse sugar.

6 Bake until crust is golden and fruit is bubbling, about 1 hour 20 minutes. Let cool slightly and serve warm with ice cream or sweetened whipped cream.

Each serving About 315 calories, 4g protein, 40g carbohydrate, 16g total fat (10g saturated), 2g fiber, 56mg cholesterol, 215mg sodium

Icy Cocktails (page 156)

Drinks

The party just got a whole lot more festive with these delicious cocktails! Stir up Lorena García's Pomegranate Passion and Café con Leche Martini, Katie Lee's Pink-Grapefruit Margaritas, Julie Morris' Superfruit Sangria, and more. Cheers!

Clinton Kelly's
Sparkling Cranberry-Cherry Punch

Total time 43 minutes   **Makes 12 cups**

Ginger Syrup
2 c. water
1½ c. sugar
**½ lb. fresh ginger, peeled
   and thinly sliced**

Gimlet Mix
2 c. fresh lime juice
2 c. Ginger Syrup

Punch
**4 c. Absolut CherryKran vodka,
   chilled**

4 c. Gimlet Mix, chilled
**¼ c. cherry syrup (from a jar
   of maraschino cherries)**
1 qt. club soda, chilled
1 lime, sliced
**1 pt. frozen cranberries
   or cherries**

1   For ginger syrup, in a large saucepan, bring sugar, water, and ginger to a boil over high heat. Reduce heat to medium and simmer 3 minutes. Remove from heat; let stand 30 minutes to steep. Strain syrup through a mesh strainer. Chill in refrigerator.

2   For gimlet mix, combine ingredients by stirring together. Chill in refrigerator.

3   Pour vodka, gimlet mix, and cherry syrup into a large punch bowl; stir to combine. Stir in club soda. Add ice cubes and garnish with fruit.

Each 1-cup serving About 304 calories, 0g protein, 35g carbohydrate, 0g total fat, 1g fiber, 0mg cholesterol, 18mg sodium

The prep work that goes into making this has a big payoff, Kelly says. "No one wants to play bartender at her own party. It inhibits mingling—the primary responsibility of a good host!"

The Tippling Bros.' Icy Cocktails

Frozen Cucumber Ginger Gimlet

Blend **¾ cup gin**; a **6-inch-long piece of English cucumber**; **1 tablespoon fresh ginger**, peeled and grated; **½ cup freshly squeezed lime juice**; *⅓ cup simple syrup* (see Lemon Basil Screamer, opposite, for recipe); and **3 cups cracked ice** until smooth. Garnish with a **slice of cucumber** and **candied ginger**.

Each serving About 190 calories, 0.5g protein, 25g carbohydrate, 0g total fat, 0.5g fiber, 0mg cholesterol, 2mg sodium

Cinnamon Bourbon Frost

For *cinnamon simple syrup*, combine **1 cup sugar, 1 cup water,** and **2 cinnamon sticks** in a saucepan. Bring to a boil for 1 minute, stirring until sugar dissolves. Reduce heat to a slow simmer for 15 minutes. Cool to room temperature. Strain cinnamon and transfer liquid to an airtight container. (Will keep in the fridge for up to 1 week.) Blend **1 cup bourbon, ¾ cup fresh raspberries,** *¾ cup cinnamon simple syrup*, **½ cup lemon juice, ¼ teaspoon Tabasco or other hot sauce** (or more to taste), and **4 cups crushed ice** until smooth.

Each serving About 243 calories, 0.5g protein, 43g carbohydrate, 0g total fat, 2g fiber, 0mg cholesterol, 3mg sodium

Lemon-Basil Screamer

For *simple syrup*, combine **1 cup sugar** and **1 cup boiling water** in a heatproof container. Allow to cool at room temperature and transfer to an airtight container. (Will keep in the fridge for up to 1 week.) Blend **¾ cup vodka, ¼ cup freshly squeezed lemon juice, ¾ cup loosely packed basil leaves,** *½ cup simple syrup*, and **3 cups crushed ice** until smooth. Pour into glass and garnish with **fresh basil leaves.**

Each serving About 198 calories, 0g protein, 26g carbohydrate, 0g total fat, 0g fiber, 0mg cholesterol, 1mg sodium

Superfood Cooler

For *honey syrup*, combine **1 cup honey** with **1 cup boiling water** in a heatproof container. Cool to room temperature and transfer to an airtight container. (Will keep in the fridge for up to 2 weeks.) Slice **1 English cucumber** in half. Slice half of the cuke into ½-inch rounds and cut the remaining half lengthwise into slices for garnish. Blend **cucumber rounds,** *½ cup honey syrup*, **1 cup blanco tequila, ½ cup freshly squeezed lemon juice, ½ cup ripe blueberries,** and **3 cups crushed ice** until smooth. Garnish with **cucumber** and a **lemon wheel.**

Each serving About 218 calories, 1g protein, 24g carbohydrate, 0g total fat, 1g fiber, 0mg cholesterol, 2mg sodium

Guy Fieri's
Big Island Punch

Total time 5 minutes

Makes 8 servings

2 c. white rum
2 c. pineapple juice
1 c. fresh lime juice

1 c. mango juice
½ c. elderflower liqueur
2 limes, sliced

1 large orange, sliced
2 c. spiced rum
¼ c. grenadine

In pitcher, mix together white rum, pineapple juice, fresh lime juice, mango juice, and elderflower liqueur. Stir in the lime and orange slices. Top with the spiced rum and grenadine. Serve over ice.

Each serving About 408 calories, 1g protein, 31g carbohydrate, 0g total fat, 2g fiber, 0mg cholesterol, 6mg sodium

Guy's Tip:
Make the punch's base, through the mango juice, up to six hours ahead.

Aarón Sánchez's Latinopolitan

Total time 5 minutes

Makes 2 servings

6 oz. light rum	2½ Tbsp. cranberry juice
1 Tbsp. agave nectar	2 mint leaves
4 Tbsp. lime juice	

Put some ice in a cocktail shaker. Add the rum, agave nectar, lime juice, and cranberry juice, and shake well. Strain into two chilled martini glasses and float a mint leaf inside.

Each serving About 240 calories, 0g protein, 13g carbohydrate, 0g total fat, 0g fiber, 0mg cholesterol, 3mg sodium

All-Star Chefs' Favorite Summertime Drinks

"Freezing-cold Prosecco with a squeeze of lemon. Does that cocktail have a name besides refreshingly delicious?"
—Alex Guarnaschelli, *Chopped* judge and Iron Chef

"Suze tonic."
—Geoffrey Zakarian, Co-Host of *The Kitchen*, *Chopped* judge, and Iron Chef

"At my restaurant Landmarc, we have a cocktail called the 'PM Kick' made with Tanteo jalapeño tequila, fresh watermelon, agave syrup, and cilantro. The flavor combination makes the perfect summer drink!"
—Marc Murphy, *Chopped* judge

"Mezcal and lime on the rocks with a side of soda water. Smoky, limey, and complex."
—Jeff Mauro, Co-Host of *The Kitchen*

"Ever since I visited Barbados last November, I've been really into Mount Gay rum. Lately, I've been mixing Mount Gay rum with coconut water, a little bit of club soda, and a splash of freshly squeezed lime juice, all garnished with a sprig of fresh mint."
—Jose Garces, Iron Chef

Julie Morris' Superfruit Sangria

Makes 4–6 servings

2 c. frozen mixed berries
¼ c. dried mulberries
¼ c. dried goldenberries, finely
    chopped

2 Tbsp. dried goji berries
1¼ c. pomegranate juice
1 bottle red wine

2 c. kombucha (unflavored or
    ginger flavored), or mineral
    water

1 Pour the fruits into a large pitcher, followed by the pomegranate juice and the wine. Refrigerate for a minimum of 5 hours or overnight to let the flavors marry—the longer the sangria sits, the better!

2 Just before serving, add the kombucha. Serve with or without ice, including some fruit in each glass.

Each serving About 231 calories, 3g protein, 33g carbohydrate, 1g total fat (0g saturated), 6g fiber, 0mg cholesterol, 25mg sodium

Superfood Tip

Using frozen and dried berries instead of fresh in this type of marinated cocktail allows the natural juices and sweet flavors of the fruit to infiltrate the beverage more effectively. Plus, the wine-infused fruit has an enhanced tenderness, providing a very pleasurable treat at the bottom of every glass.

Lorena García's Sweet Sips

Makes 1 serving

Pomegranate Passion

2 **parts bourbon**	**½** **part freshly squeezed**
1 **part pomegranate juice**	**lemon juice**
½ **part agave syrup (dark)**	**Pomegranate seeds**

Add all ingredients to a shaker filled with ice. Shake vigorously for 10 seconds. Pour over ice in a rocks glass. Garnish with pomegranate seeds.

Each serving About 223 calories, 0.5g protein, 23g carbohydrate, 0g total fat, 0.5g fiber, 0mg cholesterol, 6mg sodium

Makes 1 serving

Chiquita Rum

1½ oz. rum	**¾ oz. lime juice**
¾ oz. banana schnapps	**¾ oz. pineapple juice**
½ banana	**Splash simple syrup**
1 oz. coconut water	

Mix ingredients together in shaker with ice. Strain and serve in ice-filled martini glass.

Each serving About 260 calories, 1g protein, 31g carbohydrate, 0g total fat, 2g fiber, 0mg cholesterol, 3mg sodium

Café con Leche Martini

1 oz. freshly brewed espresso	**Splash Kahlúa**
1 oz. Frangelico	**Whipped cream**
1½ oz. premium vanilla vodka	

Pour espresso, Frangelico, vodka, and Kahlúa into shaker filled with ice. Shake until frothy and almost frozen. Strain into a chilled martini glass. Garnish with a dollop of whipped cream on top.

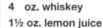

Each serving About 227 calories, 0.5g protein, 13g carbohydrate, 1g total fat (0.5g saturated), 0g fiber, 3mg cholesterol, 5mg sodium

Burbujas

4 oz. whiskey	**Ginger beer, to top**
1½ oz. lemon juice	**Lemon peel**
1 oz. simple syrup	
3 dashes Jerry Thomas' Own Decanter Bitters	

Mix ingredients, except ginger beer, in shaker. Strain into glass with ice. Top with ginger beer. Garnish with lemon peel.

Each serving About 374 calories, 0g protein, 30g carbohydrate, 0g total fat, 0g fiber, 0mg cholesterol, 2mg sodium

Lisa Lillien's
Calorie-Saving Cocktails

Green Grape Frojito

Cut a **lime** into quarters and put 2 of the quarters in a glass. Add **2 or 3 mint leaves** and **half a stevia packet;** muddle contents. In a blender, combine **¾ cup frozen green grapes, 1½ ounces rum, ¾ cup crushed ice,** and **1 tablespoon water.** Add the juice from the other 2 lime quarters, blend until smooth, and pour into glass.

Each serving About 192 calories, 1g protein, 26g carbohydrate, <0.5g total fat (0g saturated), 1.5g fiber, 0mg cholesterol, 4mg sodium

Magical Low-Calorie Margarita

Combine **6 ounces diet lemon-lime soda, 1½ ounces tequila, 1 ounce lime juice,** and **a single-serving packet of sugar-free lemonade powdered drink mix.** Stir until the drink mix dissolves, and serve over ice.

Each serving About 115 calories, 0g protein, 2g carbohydrate, 0g total fat, 0g fiber, 0mg cholesterol, 70mg sodium

Katie Lee's
Pink-Grapefruit Margaritas

Makes 6-8 servings

Lime wedge
Kosher salt
1 c. ruby red grapefruit juice

1 Tbsp. superfine sugar
2 c. triple sec
2 c. good-quality silver tequila

Ice
Grapefruit slice, cut into
    segments

1 Rub the outside rim of each margarita glass with the lime wedge. Press each glass in kosher salt to coat.

2 Combine grapefruit juice, sugar, triple sec, and tequila. Serve with ice for on the rocks, or blend with ice for frozen. Garnish with grapefruit segment.

Each serving About 353 calories, 0g protein, 29g carbohydrate, 0g total fat, 0g fiber, 0mg cholesterol, 413mg sodium

Frozen Banana Yogurt Split (page 146)

Metric Equivalents

The recipes in this book use the standard United States method for measuring liquid and dry or solid ingredients (teaspoons, tablespoons, and cups). The information in these charts is provided to help cooks outside the U.S. successfully use these recipes. All equivalents are approximate.

Metric Equivalents for Different Types of Ingredients

A standard cup measure of a dry or solid ingredient will vary in weight depending on the type of ingredient. A standard cup of liquid is the same volume for any type of liquid. Use the following chart when converting standard cup measures to grams (weight) or milliliters (volume).

Standard Cup	Fine Powder (e.g., flour)	Grain (e.g., rice)	Granular (e.g., sugar)	Liquid Solids (e.g., butter)	Liquid (e.g., milk)
1	140 g	150 g	190 g	200 g	240 ml
¾	105 g	113 g	143 g	150 g	180 ml
⅔	93 g	100 g	125 g	133 g	160 ml
½	70 g	75 g	95 g	100 g	120 ml
⅓	47 g	50 g	63 g	67 g	80 ml
¼	35 g	38 g	48 g	50 g	60 ml
⅛	18 g	19 g	24 g	25 g	30 ml

Useful Equivalents for Liquid Ingredients by Volume

¼ tsp	=						1 ml
½ tsp	=						2 ml
1 tsp	=						5 ml
3 tsp	=	1 tblsp	=	½ fl oz	=		15 ml
2 tblsp	=	⅛ cup	=	1 fl oz	=		30 ml
4 tblsp	=	¼ cup	=	2 fl oz	=		60 ml
5 ⅓ tblsp	=	⅓ cup	=	3 fl oz	=		80 ml
8 tblsp	=	½ cup	=	4 fl oz	=		120 ml
10 ⅔ tblsp	=	⅔ cup	=	5 fl oz	=		160 ml
12 tblsp	=	¾ cup	=	6 fl oz	=		180 ml
16 tblsp	=	1 cup	=	8 fl oz	=		240 ml
1 pt	=	2 cups	=	16 fl oz	=		480 ml
1 qt	=	4 cups	=	32 fl oz	=		960 ml
				33 fl oz	=		1000 ml

Useful Equivalents for Cooking / Oven Temperatures

	Fahrenheit	Celsius	Gas Mark
Freeze water	32° F	0° C	
Room temperature	68° F	20° C	
Boil water	212° F	100° C	
Bake	325° F	160° C	3
	350° F	180° C	4
	375° F	190° C	5
	400° F	200° C	6
	425° F	220° C	7
	450° F	230° C	8
Broil			Grill

Useful Equivalents for Dry Ingredients by Weight
(To convert ounces to grams, multiply the number of ounces by 30.)

1 oz	=	1/16 lb	=	30 g
4 oz	=	¼ lb	=	120 g
8 oz	=	½ lb	=	240 g
12 oz	=	¾ lb	=	360 g
16 oz	=	1 lb	=	480 g

Useful Equivalents for Length
(To convert inches to centimeters, multiply the number of inches by 2.5.)

1 in	=			2.5 cm
6 in	=	½ ft	=	15 cm
12 in	=	1 ft	=	30 cm
36 in	=	3 ft	= 1 yd	=	90 cm
40 in	=			100 cm =1m

Credits

Photo Credits

Front Cover, top row from left: © Con Poulos; © Kate Mathis; courtesy of Guy Fieri (Fieri); © Greg Powers (Hall); © Hirsheimer & Hamilton. Bottom row, from left: © Kat Teutsch (meatballs); © Peter Murdock (Lee); © Giles Ashford (Conant); © Dana Gallagher; © Marlboro Man (Drummond); © Melanie Acevedo (punch); © Susan Pittard/Studio D

Back cover, clockwise from top left: © Melanie Acevedo; © Kate Mathis (x4); © Dana Gallagher; © Jose Picayo; © John Kernick; © Jose Picayo

© Melanie Acevedo: 36, 154
© Gilles Ashford: 10 top
© Sylvie Becquet: 20 top
© Oliver Barth: 18 top
© Courtesy of Joy Bauer: 8 top
Courtesy of Beekman 1802/Paulette
   Tavormina: 34
Courtesy of Besh Resaurant Group:
   9 top, 129
© Paul Brissman: 145
© Julia Cawley/Studio D: 162, 163
Corbis: © Eric Risberg/AP Photo:
   12 bottom
© Chris Court: 63, 112, 140
© Diana DeLucia: 7 top
Courtesy of Guy Fieri: 11 bottom
© Phillip Friedman/Studio D: 28
© Dana Gallagher: 78, 102, 137
Getty Images: © Monty Brinton/CBS:
   23; © Simon Dawson/Bloomberg:
   18 bottom; © Rommel Demano: 20
   bottom; © Greg Gayne/NBC/NBCU
   Photo Bank: 10 bottom
© Steve Giralt: 2, 16 top
© Ken Goodman: 7 bottom
Courtesy of Gordon Ramsay's World
   Kitchen: 19 bottom

© Steve Hamilton: 13 top
© Brent Herris: 66
© Hirsheimer & Hamilton: 81
© Ben Hoffman: 8 bottom
Courtesy of Hungry Girl, Inc.:
   17 bottom
iStockphoto: © bhofack2: 40, 61;
   © haveseen: 160; © MmeEmil: 74
Courtesy of Stephanie Izzard:
   15 bottom
© Francis Janisch: 111
© Ray Kachatorian: 21 bottom,
   31, 46, 126
© Sam Kaplan: 91
© John Kernick: 146, 166
© John Lee: 97
Courtesy of Sandra Lee: 17
© David Loftus: 73
© Michael Lovitt: 9 bottom
© Marlboro Man: 11 top
© Kate Mathis: 4, 53, 82, 92, 124, 132,
   133, 158
© Maura McEvoy: 50
Courtesy of Andrew Meade:
   15 top, 123
© William Meppem: 14 bottom
© Johnny Miller: 26, 94, 114, 131, 151

© Julie Morris: 48, 161
© Peter Murdock: 16 bottom
© Marcus Nilsson: 86, 134
Courtesy of Daphne Oz: 19 top
© Jose Picayo: 106, 116
© Michael Pisarri: 13 bottom
© Susan Pittard/Studio D: 21 top, 38,
   45, 159
© Con Poulos: 59, 69, 70, 85, 100, 108
© Greg Powers: 14 top
© Carolyne Roehm: 43, 109
© Kate Sears: 24
Shutterstock: © Tobik: 55;
   © vetre: 64
© Paul Sirasalee: 152, 156, 157
StockFood: ©Ellen Silverman: 119
Courtesy of Michael Symon
   Restaurants: 22 top
© Chris Terry: 105, 143
© Kat Teutsch: 88
© Laura Volo: 22 bottom
© Sarah Anne Ward: 103, 164
© James Westman/Studio D: 56, 165
© Jim Wright: 12 top

Recipe Credits

Page 27; 51; 95: Stuffed French Toast; Sugar Snap Pea Salad with Pecans; and Perfect Roast Leg of Lamb from *My Family Table* by John Besh/Andrews McMeel Publishing, LLC.

Page 28; 56; 107; 117; 165: Cinnamon-Swirl Breakfast Bread Pudding; Grilled Sweet Potato and Arugula Salad; Steak Chimichurri with Grilled Tomatoes; Salmon Cakes with Artichoke Tartar Sauce; and Pink-Grapefruit Margaritas copyright © Katie Lee.

Page 31: Broccoli and Ham Strata copyright © Gale Gand.

Page 30: Hotcakes with Delicious Blueberry Compote from *Relaxed Cooking with Curtis Stone: Recipes to Put You in My Favorite* Mood by Curtis Stone, copyright ©2009 by Curtis Stone. Used by permission of Clarkson Potter/ Publishers, an imprint of the Crown Publishing Group, a division of Penguin Random House LLC. All rights reserved.

Page 32; 44; 89; 118; 146: Spiced Cranberry Coffee Cake; Queso Flameado; BBQ Sweet Tater and Chicken Enchilada Stack; Crab, Shrimp, and Goat Cheese Poblanos with Chipotle Sauce; and Frozen Banana Yogurt Split copyright © The Casserole Queens.

Page 33: Mushroom, Goat Cheese, and Tomato Tart copyright © Marcus Samuelsson Group, LLC.

Page 35; 77; 86; 134: Mini Ham and Cheese Biscuits; Grilled Summer Squash Pizza; Maple-Bourbon Roast Turkey with Gravy; and Sweet Potatoes with Ancho-Maple Glaze from *The*

Beekman 1802 Heirloom Cookbook ©2011 by Brent Ridge, Josh Kilmer-Purcell, and Sandy Gluck. Reprinted by permission of Sterling Publishing Company, Inc.

Page 39; 45; 159: Shrimp Tostadas with Salsa; Chorizo Meatballs; and Latinopolitan copyright © Aarón Sánchez.

Page 40: Party-Perfect Guacamole copyright © Chef Marcela, LLC.

Page 41; 58: Stuffed Mushrooms and Cinnamon-Spiced Sweet Potato Soup with Maple Croutons copyright © Daphne Oz.

Page 42; 109; 120: Summer Rice Croquettes; Prosciutto Pizza; and Seafood Pasta copyright © Carolyne Roehm.

Page 49; 76; 161: Roasted Vegetable Salad with Black Pepper Vinaigrette; Zucchini Fettuccine with Walnuts and Dulse; and Superfruit Sangria from *Superfood Kitchen*, text and photography ©2012 by Julie Morris. Reprinted by permission of Sterling Publishing Company, Inc.

Page 52; 130; 149: Avocado Salad with Lime and Cumin Vinaigrette; Honey-Rum Baked Black Beans; and Peach-Raspberry Crisp copyright © Bobby Flay.

Page 54; 88: Thousand Islands Dressing and Caesar Dressing [as shown in Woman's Day online, 52910] from *Your Inner Skinny* by Joy Bauer. Copyright ©2009, 2010 by Joy Bauer. Reprinted by permission of HarperCollins Publishers;

Buttermilk Ranch Dip and Joy's Turkey Meatballs [as shown in Woman's Day online, 30315] from *Slim & Scrumptious* by Joy Bauer. Copyright ©2010 by Joy Bauer. Reprinted by permission of HarperCollins Publishers.

Page 57; 127: Baja Salad and Quick-Braised Spring Vegetables from *Good Food, Good Life: 130 Simple Recipes You'll Love to Make and Eat* by Curtis Stone, copyright ©2015 by Curtis Stone. Photographs by Ray Kachatorian, copyright ©2015 by Ray Kachatorian. Used by permission of Ballantine Books, an imprint of Random House, a division of Penguin Random House LLC. All rights reserved.

Pages 60–61: Lobster Bisque from *Now Eat This!: 150 of America's Favorite Comfort Foods, All Under 350 Calories* by Rocco DiSpirito, copyright ©2010 by Spirit Media LLC. Used by permission of Ballantine Books, an imprint of Random House, a division of Penguin Random House LLC. All rights reserved.

Page 62; 85; 155: Slow Cooker White Bean Chicken Chili; Crispy Chicken and White Beans; and Sparkling Cranberry-Cherry Punch copyright © Clinton Kelly.

Page 63; 121; 141: Roasted Butternut Squash Soup; Garlic and Tarragon Shrimp; and Blueberry, Apple, and Coconut Crumble from *The New Classics* by Donna Hay. Reprinted with permission from HarperCollins Publishers.

Page 68: Corn, Zucchini, and Jalapeño Spaghetti with Parmesan Crumbs copyright © Michael Symon.

Page 71: Eggplant Caponata Subs from *America – Farm to Table: Simple, Delicious Recipes Celebrating Local Farmers* by Mario Batali and Jim Webster. Copyright ©2014 by Mario Batali LLC. Reprinted by permission of Grand Central Publishing.

Page 72: Killer Mac 'n' Cheese from *Jamie's America: Easy Twists on Great American Classics and More* by Jamie Oliver. Copyright ©2009 Jamie Oliver. Reprinted by permission of Hachette Books.

Pages 74–75: Spaghetti with Tomato Sauce from *The Scarpetta Cookbook* by Scott Conant. Copyright ©2014 by Scott Conant. Photograph copyright ©2013 by Brent Herris. Reprinted by permission of Houghton Mifflin Harcourt Publishing Company. All rights reserved.

Page 80: Mini Chicken Potpies copyright © Sandra Lee, courtesy sandralee.com.

Pages 82–83; 98; 158: California Brick Chicken with Apricot-Mint Chimichurri; St. Louis Ribs with Tequila BBQ Sauce; and Guy's Big Island Punch [as printed in Good Housekeeping magazine, June 2014] from *Guy on Fire: 130 Recipes for Adventures in Outdoor Cooking* by Guy Fieri and Ann Volkwein. Copyright ©2011 by Guy Fieri. Reprinted by permission of HarperCollins Publishers.

Page 84: Skillet Chicken, Potatoes, and Peppers from *Lidia's Family Table* by Lidia Matticchio Bastianich with David Nussbaum, copyright ©2004 by Tutti a Tavola, LLC. Used by permission of Alfred A. Knopf, an imprint of Knopf Doubleday Publishing Group, a division of Penguin Random House LLC. All rights reserved.

Page 90: Buffalo Wing Burgers from *Cooking with Love: Comfort Food That Loves You* by Carla Hall. Text copyright ©2012 by Carla Hall. Reprinted by permission of Atria Books, a Division of Simon & Schuster, Inc.

Page 96: California Osso Buco with Kumquat-Cranberry Gremolata reprinted from *Tyler Florence Family Meal* by Tyler Florence. Copyright ©2010 by Tyler Florence. Permission granted by Rodale Inc., Emmaus, PA 18098.

Page 99: Pork Chops with Sage from *Jamie's Italy* by Jamie Oliver. Copyright ©2005 Jamie Oliver. Reprinted by permission of Hachette Books.

Page 101; 135: Grilled Steak with Stone-Fruit Tapenade and Baby Summer Squash with Ricotta and Mint copyright © Stephanie Izard.

Page 102: Root Beer-Glazed Ham from *The Pioneer Woman Cooks: A Year of Holidays* by Ree Drummond. Copyright ©2013 by Ree Drummond. Reprinted by permission of HarperCollins Publishers.

Page 103: Pork-Apricot Fried Rice, and photograph by Andrew Meade, from *Latin D'Lite: Delicious Latin Recipes with a Healthy Twist* by Ingrid Hoffmann, translated by Angelina Garcia, copyright ©2013 by Ingrid Hoffmann. Used by permission of Celebra, an imprint of Penguin Publishing Group, a division of Penguin Random House LLC.

Page 104; 142–143: Blue Cheese Burgers and Boston Cream Pie from *Gordon Ramsay's World Kitchen* (Quadrille Publishing) by Gordon Ramsay. Copyright © Gordon Ramsay.

Page 108: Sausage with Lentils and Spinach, courtesy of Mario Batali.

Page 110; 131; 150: Poppy-Seed Pork Tenderloin with a Fresh Herb Crust; Sweet Corn and Tomato Relish; and Peach Cobbler from *Carla's Comfort Foods* by Carla Hall. Copyright ©2014 by Carla Hall. Photograph for Poppy-Seed Pork Tenderloin with a Fresh Herb Crust copyright ©2014 by Frances Janisch. Reprinted by permission of Atria Books, a Division of Simon & Schuster, Inc.

Page 115: Trout Almondine from *Besh Big Easy* by John Besh/Andrews McMeel Publishing, LLC.

Page 122: Chicharrones Fish Tacos with Chipotle Tartar Sauce copyright © Chica Worldwide LLC.

Page 128: Tomatoes with Crabmeat from *My New Orleans* by John Besh/Andrews McMeel Publishing, LLC.

Page 136; 148: Herbed Potatoes au Gratin and Lemon Blueberry Layer Cake copyright © Ree Drummond.

Page 144: Spiced Apple Pie with Cheddar Crust from *Marcus Off Duty: The Recipes I Cook at Home* by Marcus Samuelsson with Roy Finamore. Copyright ©2014 by Marcus Samuelsson Group LLC. Photograph ©2014 by Paul Brissman. Reprinted by permission of Houghton Mifflin Harcourt Publishing Company. All rights reserved.

Pages 156–157: Frozen Cucumber Ginger Gimlet; Cinnamon Bourbon Frost; Lemon-Basil Screamer; and Superfood Cooler copyright © Tad Carducci and Paul Tanguay.

Pages 162–163: Pomegranate Passion; Chiquita Rum; Café con Leche Martini; and Burbujas copyright © Lorena García.

Page 164: Green Grape Frojito and Magical Low-Calorie Margarita copyright © by Lisa Lillien. Reprinted by permission of Sterling Lord Literistic, Inc.

Index

HEARSTBOOKS

An Imprint of Sterling Publishing
1166 Avenue of the Americas
New York, NY 10036

ISBN 978-1-61837-214-7

Distributed in Canada by Sterling Publishing
c/o Canadian Manda Group, 664 Annette Street
Toronto, Ontario, Canada M6S 2C8
Distributed in the United Kingdom by GMC Distribution Services
Castle Place, 166 High Street, Lewes, East Sussex, England BN7 1XU
Distributed in Australia by Capricorn Link (Australia) Pty. Ltd.
P.O. Box 704, Windsor, NSW 2756, Australia

For information about custom editions, special sales, and premium and
corporate purchases, please contact Sterling Special Sales at 800-805-5489
or specialsales@sterlingpublishing.com.

Project Editor: Andrea Modica
Book Design: Anna Christian

Manufactured in China

2 4 6 8 10 9 7 5 3 1

www.sterlingpublishing.com